A NOTEBOOK ON
WILLIAM SHAKESPEARE

A Notebook on
WILLIAM
SHAKESPEARE

BY

EDITH SITWELL
Hon. D.Litt. (Leeds), Hon. D.Litt. (Durham)

LONDON
MACMILLAN & CO. LTD
1948

TO
ARTHUR WALEY
AND
BERYL DE ZOETE

FOREWORD

THIS is my *Notebook*, like the *Poet's Notebook* published in 1943, and it contains, in addition to my own Notes, copious quotations from Shakespearean scholars, and passages from other works which seem to me applicable to this subject.

With the exception of the passages on *Macbeth*, *King Lear*, and *Othello*, the book consists of a series of notes, which are not to be considered as essays, but rather as running commentaries on certain aspects of Shakespeare.

These were written with a proper sense of humility, and awe of my subject.

I have not written of all the plays, nor is there a chronological arrangement.

E. S.

ACKNOWLEDGMENTS

MY most grateful thanks are due to the following authors, translators, editors, and publishers, all of whom have treated me with the greatest kindness.

The executors of the late Mr. Harley Granville-Barker and Messrs. Sidgwick & Jackson for permission to include an extract from *Prefaces to Shakespeare*. To Mr. M. A. Bayfield and the Cambridge University Press for the extract from *A Study of Shakespeare's Versification*. To Mr. Edmund Blunden and Messrs. Jonathan Cape for the passages from *The Mind's Eye*. To the executors of the late Dr. A. C. Bradley and Messrs. Macmillan for the passages from *Shakespearean Tragedy*. To Sir Edmund Chambers and the Clarendon Press for the quotations from *William Shakespeare*. To Mrs. F. M. Cornford and Messrs. Edward Arnold for the quotations from the late Dr. F. M. Cornford's *The Origin of Attic Comedy*. To Mrs. Laurence Binyon and Messrs. Macmillan for permission to include lines from the late Mr. Binyon's translation of Dante's *The Inferno*. To Mr. Mark van Doren and Messrs. Allen & Unwin for the quotations from *The Plays of Shakespeare*. To the executors of the late Professor Edward Dowden and the Oxford University Press for a quotation from the Prefaces to the Oxford Edition of *Shakespeare*. To Mr. Lewis Richard Farnell and the Clarendon Press for permission to quote from *Cults of the Greek States*. To Mrs. James Joyce and Messrs. John Lane, The Bodley Head, for permission to include an extract from the late Mr. James Joyce's *Ulysses*. To Dr. C. G. Jung, his translator Mr. Stanley Dell, and Messrs. Kegan Paul for permission to quote a passage from *The Integration of the Personality*. To Dr. Gilbert Murray, O.M., Sir Idris Bell, C.B., O.B.E., and the Oxford University Press for permission to quote from Dr. Murray's *Hamlet and Orestes* (annual Shakespeare Lecture for the British Academy, 1914); and to Dr. Murray and Messrs. Allen & Unwin for the lines from Dr. Murray's translation of Euripides' *Hippolytus*. To Mr. Francis Maitland and Messrs. Thomas Nelson & Sons for the excerpts from Henri Poincaré's *Science and Method* (translated by Mr. Maitland). To the executors of the late Sir James Frazer, O.M., and Messrs. Macmillan for the passages from Pausanias' *Description of Greece* ; and to the executors of the late Sir Arthur Quiller-Couch and the Cambridge University Press for passages from *Shakespeare's Workmanship* and the Preface to *All's Well that Ends Well* (the Cambridge Edition of *Shakespeare*). To Mr. Harold Rosenberg and the Editor of *View* for the passages from *Notes on Identity*, with special reference to the Mixed Philosopher, Soren Kierkegaard : *View*, May 1946. To Mr. Stephen Spender and the Editor of *New Writing*, for permission to quote the passages on *Macbeth* from Penguin *New Writing*, No. 6. To Dr. Caroline Spurgeon and the Clarendon Press for permission to quote from *Imagery in Shakespeare*. To Dr. E. M. W. Tillyard, Master of Jesus College, Cambridge, and to Messrs. Chatto & Windus for the passages from *The Elizabethan World Picture* and *Shakespeare's History Plays*. And to Mr. Edward MacCurdy and Messrs. Duckworth for the passage from Mr. MacCurdy's translation of Leonardo da Vinci's *Note-Book*.

For all the great kindness shown me by these authors, translators, editors, and publishers, I am deeply grateful.

If by any inadvertence I have used any copyright material for which permission was not asked, or have failed to return thanks where thanks are due, I offer my very sincere apologies, which I hope will be accepted by those concerned.

I must also thank the Editor of *New Writing* and *Daylight* for his kind permission to include the essay on *King Lear*, and the Notes on Iago, which appeared, first, in *New Writing*; the Editor of the *Nineteenth Century and After* for permission to include the essay on *Measure for Measure*, and the Editor of *View* for permission to quote a large part of the essay on *Macbeth*, many of the General Notes, and the Notes on " Clams and Fools ", which appeared, first, in *View*.

My most grateful thanks are due, also, to Miss F. E. Woolford, who has kindly undertaken the secretarial work connected with this book, and whose invaluable help has been beyond praise.

E. S.

CONTENTS

I

THE HYMN TO LIFE

In these gigantic works, there are the differences in nature, in matter, in light, in darkness, in movement, that we find in the universe.

Sometimes the identities of which the world is composed belong, as it were, to the different grades in the series of existence, — to the mineral kingdom, the vegetable kingdom, the brute creation. Or they are one of the elements : Water : Hamlet. Air : Romeo and Juliet. Fire : Lear. (Goethe said that ' Time is an element '. Time may be said to be the other element in Lear, of whom Coleridge said ' old age is a character '. But in King Lear, the character is more than old age : it is Time itself. Time is the essence of Lear's being, the space in which that being exists.) The fourth element, Earth, is always present. Shakespeare knew that there is no fragment of clay, however little worth, that is not entirely composed of inexplicable qualities.

Characters such as Falstaffe are ' lumps of the world ', ' are still alive from the roots, a part not yet cut off from universal nature ', and they have a gross physical enormity of sensation which approaches a kind of physical godhead.

Shakespeare is like the sun, that common-kissing Titan, having a passion for matter, pure and impure, an energy beyond good and evil, an immense benevolence creating without choice or preference, out of the need of giving birth to life. ' Never was there such a homage to light, to light and the principle of life.' [1]

Antony swears

By the fire
That quickens Nilus' slime.

---

[1] This was said by Arthur Symons of a still great, though infinitely lesser artist than Shakespeare, and an artist in a different medium — Édouard Manet. But it seems still more applicable to Shakespeare.

Poor Pompey, the bawd's tapster in *Measure for Measure*, excuses himself to his judge by saying :

> Truly, sir, I am a poor fellow that would live.

And Shakespeare, if no one else, forgives him, for to Shakespeare life is holy, and Pompey, Mrs. Quickly, and other earthy characters, of this, as of every other kind, hold in them the principle, and the love, of life. These, and Nilus' slime, are worthy in his eyes of the light and heat of the sun.

> None does offend, none, I say, none ;

said the old mad King upon the dark moor. And so said his loving creator. The terrible storms of the most gigantic tragedies ever born from the heart of Man, though they are vast as the upheavals of Nature, are not blind as these. It is no fault of the sun if we wreck our world. . . . In *King Lear*, in *Timon of Athens*, the diatribes are only the reverse side of love.

' We are really for brief moments Primordial Being itself, and feel its indomitable desire for being, and joy in existence. The struggle, the pain, the destruction of phenomena appear to us something necessary . . . considering the fertility of the universal will.' [1]

' There's sap in it yet ', says Antony to his Queen before darkness falls. Sap in the event, sap in the heart of Man.

Old Falstaffe, with his heat and intemperance, his love of life, is to Shakespeare, as to Prince Hal, '. . . thou latter spring . . . all hallow'en summer '.

Only that which is too cold for Hell (as was, perhaps, Iago, once a native) is condemned. Only the hard heart offends. But this, too, though it is more inflexible than marble or than the cold of death, must be investigated.

' Then let them anatomise Regan,' said the old outcast King, ' see what breeds about her heart. Is there any cause

---

[1] Nietzsche, *The Birth of Tragedy*.

in Nature that makes these hard hearts ? '

To Shakespeare, generation and the processes of generation, Death and the processes of Death, are holy.

In these hymns to Life, the very blood of the beings, the
animate heat, is spirit. . . . ' Not fire, it does not take its
origin from fire, but derives from the solar ray. . . . The
blood acquires remarkable and most excellent powers, and
is analogous to the stars. . . .'

' The heat of the sun and of animals,[1] not only that
which is stored up in semen, but even that of any excre-
mentitious matter, although divers in nature, still contains
a vital principle.' ' Now,' continues Harvey, ' I maintain
the same thing of the innate heat of the blood. I say
that they are not fire and they do not derive their origin
from fire. They rather share the nature of some other,
and that a more divine body or substance. They act
by no faculty or property of the elements; but as there is
something inherent in the semen which makes it prolific,
and as in producing an animal, it surpasses the power of
the elements — as it is a spirit, namely, and the inherent
nature of that spirit corresponds to the element of the stars,
so there is a spirit, a certain force, inherent in the blood,
acting superiorly to the powers of the elements . . . and
the nature, yea, the soul in this spirit and blood is identical
with the nature of the stars.'

In beings like Othello, the blood, ' by reason of its
admirable properties and powers, is spirit. It is celestial,
something analogous to heaven, vicarious of heaven . . .
the innate heat, the sun of the microcosm, the fire of
Plato. . . .' In such beings as Juliet's nurse, ' in so far as it
is spirit, it is the hearth, the Vesta, the household divinity '.[2]

That splendour of the blood ran through all grand
animal nature, — in that ' globe of sinful continents ', poor
old Sir John Falstaffe, the ' honeysuckle villain ', the ' honey

---

[1] Aristotle, quoted by William Harvey, *On Generation.*
[2] William Harvey, *op. cit.*

seed rogue ', whose heart was killed because a King, in whose word he had trusted, seemed to break faith with him.

It runs in the veins of the Dauphin's horse, that being of air and fire.

DAUPHIN : What a long Night is this ! I will not change my Horse with any that treades but on foure pasternes : Ça ha ! he bounds from the Earth, as if his entrayles were hayres : *le Cheval volant*, the Pegasus, *chez les narines de feu*! When I bestryde him, I soare, I am a Hawke : he trots the ayre ; the Earth sings when he touches it ; the basest horne of his hoofe is more Musicall than the Pipe of Hermes.

ORLEANS : Hee's of the colour of the Nutmeg.

DAUPHIN : And of the heat of the Ginger. It is a Beast for Perseus : hee is pure Ayre and Fire ; and the dull elements of Earth and Water never appeare in him, but only in patient stillnesse while his Rider mounts him : hee is indeed a Horse ; and all other Jades you may call Beasts.

CONSTABLE : Indeed, my Lord, it is a most absolute and excellent Horse.

DAUPHIN : It is the Prince of Palfrayes, his Neigh is like the bidding of a Monarch, and his countenance enforces Homage.

(*The Life of King Henry the Fifth*, III, 7)

Such plays as *King Henry the Fourth* (Parts I and II) and *King Henry the Fifth* are giant hymns to the physical glory of Life, and the characters seem ' the animalisation of God '.

. . . banish plumpe Jacke, and banish all the World.

(First Part of *King Henry the Fourth*, II, 4)

(That round berry the world, with its sweetness . . . the world with its earthiness and juice ; the old happy laughing world that forgets it must die.)

' Thou knowest,' said the ' honeysuckle villain ', ' in the state of Innocency Adam fell : and what would poore Jacke Falstaffe do in the dayes of Villainy ? Thou seest, I have more flesh than another man, and therefore more frailty ' (Part I, III, 3). ' . . . If Sacke and Sugar be a fault, Heaven helpe the wicked : if to be old and merry be a sinne, then many an olde Hoste that I know is damned.'

He was sinful, yes, but not diabolic.

Throughout the days of that 'latter spring . . . all hallow'en summer' (as the Prince called the old man) the sun danced, although 'the fortune of us that are the Moone's men doeth ebbe and flow like the Sea, being governed as the Sea is by . . . the Moone' (First Part of *King Henry the Fourth*, I, 2).

The hours go by, but nobody cares. The shades of night seem companions of these 'Dianae's Forresters, gentlemen of the Shade, minions of the Moone'.

Certain characters that we do not see, but that are known to the beings of this world — Robin Nightwork, for instance, and old Jane Nightwork (' old, old, Master Shallow ') and Cousin Silence whom we do see — are like sweet shadows, remembered from youth, and still haunting the brain of that earthy old man, Sir John Falstaffe, whose redness is from Adam !

Stupidity and lean Virtue are only shadows, too, but these will soon pass away under the great dancing sun, or they are a cool resting-place for laughter :

SHALLOW : For the other, Sir John : Let me see : Simon Shadow !
FALSTAFFE : I marry, let me have him to sit under : he's like to be a cold souldier.
SHALLOW : Where's Shadow ?
SHADOW : Heere, sir.

. . . . . .

SHALLOW : Do you like him, Sir John ?
FALSTAFFE : Shadow will serve for Summer : pricke him : For we have a number of shadowes to fill up the Muster-Booke.
(Second Part of *King Henry the Fourth*, III, 2)

But the shade of Sir John Falstaffe 'partook' as da Vinci said Shadow must do, ' of the nature of universal matter '.

It is better to be a fat old man ' who sweates to death, And Lards the leane earth as he walkes along ' (First Part

of *King Henry the Fourth*, II, 2), than to be Nothingness.
What is Honour ? It may lead to Nothingness, therefore
it, too, is only a shade :

> What is that Honour? Ayre. A trim reckoning ! Who
> hath it ? He that dy'de o' Wednesday. Doth he feele
> it ? No. Doth he heare it ? No. Is it insensible then ?
> Yea, to the dead. But will it not live with the living ? No.
> Why ? Detraction will not suffer it. Therefore Ile none of
> it. Honour is a meere Scutcheon, and so ends my Catechisme.
> (First Part of *King Henry the Fourth*, V, 1)

. . . A scutcheon, a ' ghost in marble ', or a shadow.
What is Honour to a ' honeysuckle villain ', in a world that
must have seemed to him, as to the Archbishop in *King
Henry the Fifth*, one of ' Singing masons building roofs
of gold '.

Falstaffe, in his instinctive life, is like ' the old noontide
sleeping. It moves its mouth. Doth it not drink a drop
of happiness, an old brown drop of golden happiness,
golden wine ? . . .' He is ' a well of eternity . . . the
joyous, awful noontide abyss '.[1]

[1] Nietzsche, *Thus Spake Zarathustra.*

II

OF THE CLOWNS AND FOOLS

' Music ', said Wagner, ' blots out our entire civilisation, as sunshine does lamplight.'

This is true of the giant harmonies of Shakespeare. In another kind, his poetry is a sun whose light does not blot out a civilisation, but fuses it into a single being.

In the Comedies, the Sun forgives and remakes the shape of evil, dances, laughing and loving the world, over stupidity.

We see the nettle-dull Dogberry and Verges. Shakespeare reduces their sheer nonsense, their incomprehension and rustic fears, into Chaos ; and then from Chaos he produces a dancing star.

When Dogberry enquires (at the beginning of the Second Scene of the Fourth Act of *Much Ado about Nothing*) :

> Is our whole dissembly appeared ?

or says :

> Write down, that they hope they serve God : and write God first ; for God defend but that God should go before such villains ! Masters, it is proved already that you are little better than false knaves, and it will go near to be thought so shortly . . . (IV, 2),

— or when Bottom the Weaver declares that the ballad about his dream ' shall be called " Bottom's Dream ", because it hath no bottom ' — (*A Midsummer-Night's Dream*, IV, 1) — we feel as if we were suddenly made conscious of ' a deformation undergone by all bodies carried forward by the earth's motion ', or, going still further, had found ourselves in a universe reigned over ' by any deformation whatsoever, — in accordance with any laws, as complicated as we liked ', — ' these laws ruling over our bodies also, and the rays of light emanating from the different objects '.[1]

Outraged by being called ' an Asse ', Dogberry cries : ' Dost thou not suspect my place ? Dost thou not suspect my yeeres ? O that hee were here to write me downe an asse ! But masters, remember that I am an asse ; though it be not written down, yet forget not that I am an asse ' (*Much Ado about Nothing*, IV, 2). And from the word ' yeeres ' we see the long ears of the Ass growing.

(' O Dionysos divine, why dost thou pull mine ears ? ' Ariadne asks her philosophical lover in one of the celebrated dialogues on the Isle of Naxos (Nietzsche). ' I find there is something agreeable, something pleasant about thine ears. . . . Why are they not still longer ? ' [2])

We are, in short, in the Fourth Dimension, — ' offering itself to the intellect from the plastic point of view, — the immensity of space eternalising itself in all directions at a determined moment. It is space itself, the dimension of the infinite ; it is this which endows objects with plasticity. It gives them, in a word, the proportions that they desire.' [3]

Sometimes, amid the Titanic dust, the Titanic heat, a strange figure is thrown, that of the ancestor of Ancient Pistol and the Capitano of Italian Comedy. This shadow has drifted down the ages to us, escaped from the campaigns of Alexander, — retaining still his bluster, his tragic bombast, and with his tremendous crest of plumes (or ' boastard's feathers ', as an enemy, Dikaiopolis, called that crest) still erect on his helmet.[4]

This being turns towards us, and we see, under the crest of feathers that is the mark of the soldier of fortune, a stock mask of Comedy, with empty eyes and open mouth — and,

[1] Henri Poincaré, *Science and Method.*
[2] Guillaume Apollinaire, *Les Peintres artistes.*
[3] Apollinaire, *op. cit.*
[4] See F. M. Cornford, *The Origin of Attic Comedy*, chapter 8, ' The Stock Mask of the Old Comedy '.

through these apertures, gain a glimpse of the face of Æschylus.[1] Sometimes, again, some being turns, and we see, not the ' Silenus-like figure and countenance, with its prominent eyes and snub nose ',[2] of the true Socrates, but the lean black shadow, with hooked nose, ' the pretended Comedy Mask of this philosopher,[3] affixed to the stock figure of the learned Doctor, ancestor of Il Dottore in Italian Comedy, and of the schoolmaster Holofernes, to whom, with his friend the Parson Sir Nathaniel, Goodman Dull, the Constable, plays buffoon '.[4]

These faces, that of Æschylus and of Socrates, as they were seen by Aristophanes, strangely wried by the Comedy masks into which they were thrust, are seen by us for a moment, brought into fresh life by the greatest of all human creators. Then the Titanic dust of all the summers that have passed since their birth, drifts round them again : and the high voice of the Clown is heard — the Ritual Laughter.

The Ritual Laughter

There are various kinds of the greater Laughter — of the Ritual or Sacred Laugh. We may study the origin and the nature of these, in Salomon Reinach's *Cultes, mythes, et religions*.

There is the laughter inspiring fear — the braying of the world of asses following the army of Darius, which, causing terror (because of the unknown, uncouth quality of the sound) among the horses of the Scythian hordes, who heard it for the first time, led to the flight of the horses and the defeat of the Scythians.—There is the laughter of those who

[1] Descended to us from Aristophanes' *The Frogs*.
[2] F. M. Cornford, *op. cit.*
[3] Polonius is, in some sense, a descendant of this mock philosopher.— E. S.
[4] ' When you see Socrates brought upon the stage, you are not to imagine him made ridiculous by the imitation of his actions,' said Dryden, in *Dramatic Poesy*, ' but rather by making him perform something very unlike himself, something so childish and absurd, as by comparing it with the gravity of the true Socrates, makes it a ridiculous object for the spectators.'

have escaped from an earthquake and find themselves in known fields.—There is the laughter which represents the return to life of the Goddess of Vegetation.—And there is the pure laughter of the God, the manifestation in sound of his presence.

' It was said ', wrote Reinach, ' that Caligula wished to transport to Rome the Zeus of Phidias, from the Olympia : the scaffoldings, the machinery, were already erected, when the statue broke into loud laughter, so that the terrified workmen took to flight.   This laughter of Zeus was not caused by the attempted sacrilege of Caligula . . . but it was the solemn affirmation, the manifestation in sound, of the presence of the God.' [1]

The terrible laughter of Hamlet seems akin to that of the young men during the Rites of the Roman Lupercalia, — who, after they had been sacrificed by proxy, were obliged, as a part of the ceremony, to break into laughter, to show that their sacrifice was completed, and that they had passed beyond death.

It is this laughter that we hear, perhaps, in certain of Hamlet's speeches.

Sometimes the laughter of Hamlet is of this kind — sometimes of the sort of which Baudelaire wrote in *Curiosités esthétiques* : ' Il est certain . . . que le rire humain est intimement lié à l'accident d'une chute ancienne, d'une dégradation physique et morale.   Le rire et la douleur s'expriment par les organes où résident le commandement et la science du bien ou du mal : les yeux et la bouche. Dans le paradis terrestre . . . (c'est-à-dire dans le milieu où il semblait à l'homme que toutes les choses créés étaient bonnes), la joie n'etait pas dans le rire.   Aucune peine ne l'affligeant, son visage etait simple et uni, et le rire qui agite maintenant les nations ne déformait pas les traits de sa face.

---

[1] ' O the rich contrast between the Clown and Hamlet, as two extremes !   You see in the former the mockery of logic, and [in the Clowns] a traditional wit valued, like truth, for its antiquity, and treasured up, like a tune, for use.'— COLERIDGE, *Lectures*, 1818.

. . . L'Être qui voulut multiplier son image, n'a point mis
dans la bouche de l'homme les dents du lion, mais l'homme
mord avec le rire.

.   .   .   .

'Le rire est . . . essentiellement contradictoire, c'est-à-
dire qu'il est à la fois signe d'une grandeur infinie et d'une
misère infinie, misère infinie relativement aux animaux.
C'est du choc perpétuel de ces deux infinis qui se dégage
le rire.'

Then, too, there is the grosser, more earthy, laughter.

> . . . broad as ten thousand beeves at pasture,
> Thunders of laughter, clearing air and heart,[1]

— the laughter of fertility at the thought of unfertility, —
the laughter of life and growth arising out of the earth that
hides the dead.

And over and through the laughter sounds the ' tuneful
planetting ' of the verse.

.   .   .   .

Foolery like the Sun

' Foolery, sir, does walke about the Orbe like the Sunne ;
it shines every where ' — said Feste.

And all the characters of the Fools have ' dimensions
that are half-way between those of an atom and those of
a star '.

When John Ray, the great 17th-century naturalist, was
asked, ' What is the use of butterflies ? ' he replied, ' To
adorn the world and delight the eyes of men, to brighten
the countryside, serving like so many golden spangles, to
decorate the fields '. And he added, ' Who can contem-
plate their exquisite beauty and not acknowledge and adore
the traces of divine art upon them ? '

[1] Sir Arthur Quiller-Couch's foreword to *All's Well that End's Well*, Cambridge
Edition Shakespeare.

The Watteau Gilles, Pierrot, is of this kind . . . (' Je vécus, étincelle d'or de la lumière nature ') . . . a simple creature adorning the world, and soon to die. The Fool in *King Lear* was once such a being.

It was Coleridge's opinion (reported by Crabbe Robinson) that the Fools of Shakespeare supplied the place of the ancient Chorus. . . . 'In *Hamlet*', he added, ' the Fool, as it were, is divided into several parts, dispersed through the play.'

The ancient wisdom, disguised as laughter, dances like the light of a great summer sea. So it is with Feste. Or it rises, in rustic disguise, like some bearded god of the ripe fig trees, from the very earth of Death :

> I wish you all joy of the Worme.
>
> (*Antony and Cleopatra*, V, 2)

Or it turns black and terrible, as if lightning-struck, as in *Hamlet* :

FIRST CLOWN : Come, my Spade : there is no ancient gentlemen but Gardiners, Ditchers, and Grave-makers ; they hold up Adam's profession.

> . . . . .

What is he that builds stronger than either the Mason, the Shipwright, or the Carpenter ?

> . . . . .

A Grave-maker : the Houses that he makes last till Doomesday.

> (*Hamlet*, V, 1)

Or again, we have ' the true man, the bearded satyr, shouting joyfully to his god '.[1] Such is Dromio of Syracuse, invoking the comfort of his master, because he is pursued by Nature, by the Earth in the shape of a kitchen wench : ' No longer from head to foot than from hippe to hippe :

---

[1] Nietzsche, *The Birth of Tragedy*.

she is sphericall, like a globe : I could find out Countries
in her '.

. . . . . .

ANTIPHOLUS OF SYRACUSE : Where Spain ?
DROMIO OF SYRACUSE : Faith, I saw it not : but I felt it in her
  breath.
ANTIPHOLUS OF SYRACUSE : Where America, the Indies ?
DROMIO OF SYRACUSE : O, sir, upon her nose : all ore embellished
  with Rubies, Carbuncles, Saphires, declining their rich
  Aspect to the hot breath of Spaine, who sent whole Armadoes
  of Caracks to be ballast at her nose.

(The Comedy of Errors, III, 2)

Round these beings, the air sparkles like a sea. And
indeed, Dromio of Syracuse and Dromio of Ephesus seem
like two strange sea-creatures, shining with the sea-jewellery.
But they come alive as we watch them and listen to them.

' When I had taken up what I had supposed to be a
fallen star,' wrote Dryden, in the Epistle Dedicatory to *The
Spanish Friar*, ' I found I had been cozened with a jelly ;
nothing but a cold, dull mass, which glittered no longer than
it was shooting ; a dwarfish mass, dressed up in gigantic
words.'

He spoke of the disappointment experienced when
reading certain plays, which he had enjoyed upon the stage.
But with Shakespeare, every shooting star remains a star,
no matter whence it is seen.

Other clowns, such as poor Pompey, the bawd's tapster,
in *Measure for Measure*, have a strange animal character —
that of the beast of burden turned prophet or soothsayer.

Dr. C. G. Jung, in *Psychology of the Unconscious*, speaks of
legends in which ' the Horse acquires the significance of the
Animal Unconscious, which appears domesticated and subjected to the will of Man '.

It is this ' Animal Unconscious ' which speaks through
the lips of Pompey, when, all unknowing, he utters words
which tell us of the great mercy of Christ.

The giant dances, and grandeur is the air, the climate, through which the storm of his footsteps sound :

BOY :   Do you not remember, a saw a Flea sticke upon Bardolph's Nose, and a said it was a Blacke Soul burning in Hell-fire ?

BARDOLPH :   Well, the fuel is gone that maintain'd that fire : that's all the Riches I got in his service.

(King Henry the Fifth, II, 3)

And Falstaffe :

> Doe thou amend thy Face, and Ile amend my Life : thou art our Admirall, thou bearest the Lanterne in the Poope, but 'tis in the Nose of thee ; thou art the Knight of the Burning Lampe.

BARDOLPH :   Why, Sir John, my Face does you no harme.

FALSTAFFE :   No, Ile be sworne ; I make as good use of it as many a man doth of a Death's Head in a Memento Mori : I never see thy Face, but I think upon Hell-fire, and Dives that lived in Purple ; for there he is in his robes, burning, burning. If thou wert any way given to vertue, I would sweare by thy Face ; my oath should bee ' By this Fire, that's God's angel ' : but thou art altogether given over ; and wert indeede, but for the Light in thy Face, the Sunne of utter Darknesse. When thou ran'st up Gads Head in the Night to catch my Horse, if I did not thinke that thou hadst beene an Ignis Fatuus or a Ball of Wild-fire, there's no Purchase in Mony.

(First Part of King Henry the Fourth, III, 3)

Gold is inherent in all natures. We see the buried, undreamt-of treasure in the smile of gravity.

' He doth smile his face into more lines than are in the new Map, with the augmentation of the Indies,' said Maria of Malvolio.

III

NOTE ON COMEDY AND TRAGEDY

(*Coleridge : Lectures*, 1818)

'. . . IN the old comedy the very form itself is whimsical;
the whole work is one great jest, comprehending a world
of jests within it, among which each maintains its own
place without seeming to concern itself as to the relation
in which it may stand to its fellows. In short, in Sophocles
the constitution of tragedy is monarchical, but such as it
existed in early Greece, limited by laws, and therefore the
more venerable — all the parts adapting and submitting
themselves to the majesty of the heroic sceptre :—in Aristophanes, comedy, on the contrary, is poetry in its most
democratic form, and it is a fundamental principle with it,
rather to risk all the confusion of anarchy, than to destroy
the interdependence and privileges of its individual constitu-
encies — verse, characters, even single thoughts, conceits
and illusions, each turning on the pivot of its own free will.

. . . .

'The comic poet idealises character by making the
animal the governing power, and the intellectual the real
instrument.

. . . .

'The sportive ideal . . . consists in the perfect harmony
and concord of the higher nature with the animal, as with
its ruling principle and its acknowledged regent.

. . . .

'An old critic said that tragedy was the flight or elevation of life, comedy (that of Menander), its arrangement
or ordonnance.

. . . .

'The old tragedy moved in an ideal world, the old
comedy in a fantastic world.'

15

IV

SOME GENERAL NOTES ON THE TRAGEDIES

'ALL is indiscriminately stamped with grandeur', as Fuseli said of Michelangelo. 'A beggar rose from his hand the patriarch of poverty; the hump of his dwarf is impressed with dignity' . . . 'the hump and withered arm of Richard are engines of terror and persuasion in Shakespeare' as 'the crook-back of Michelangelo strikes with awe'.

Thus, when Richard the Third says

> Shine out, fair Sunne, till I have bought a glasse,
> That I may see my Shadow as I passe (I, 2),

although he is speaking only of his image in a mirror, we feel, not only Richard's indifference to darkness or light, excepting inasmuch as they enhance his being, or aid him in his purpose : but we feel, also, that in the end the shadow of his hump, the shade of his withered arm, will blot out the sun.

Shakespeare knew all differences in good and evil — that between the evil of Iago, who, though a subterranean devil, is also ' Prince of the Power of the Air ' (' as the air works upon our bodies, this Presence works upon our minds '), and that of Titus Andronicus, the kind of being of whom Donne, in his 41st Sermon, said, ' He is a devil in himself, that could be, and would be, ambitious in a spital, licentious in a wilderness, voluptuous in a famine, and abound with temptations in himself, though there were no devil '. (This is not one of Shakespeare's greatest plays, but has, as Swinburne said of Chapman, ' passages of a sublime and Titanic beauty, rebellious and excessive in style as in sentiment, but full of majestic and massive harmony '.)

Certain characters in Shakespeare have the grandeur and loneliness of a pariah sun in a heaven of evil, casting down disastrous rays upon all alike, breeding new forms of life from primeval mud.

For the mud exists, but so does Beauty, ' a lively harmony, a glittering brightness, resulting from effused good by ideas, seeds, reasons, shadows, stirring up our minds that by this good they may be united and made one '.[1]

Darkness fell because of Helen, and yet she is seen as

> . . . a Grecian queen, whose youth and freshness
> Wrinkles Appolloe's, and makes stale the morning.
>
> (*Troilus and Cressida*, II, 2)

The faults of the hero have a planetary splendour :

LEPIDUS

> . . . I must not think there are
> Evils enow to darken all his goodnesse ;
> His faults in him seeme as the Spots of Heaven,
> More fiery by night's Blacknesse.
>
> (*Antony and Cleopatra*, I, 4)

Old age in Shakespeare is of a profound grandeur, though the kiss of Age brings winter even to the lips of Beauty :

> Ile take that winter from your lips, faire lady :

says Achilles to Cressida, after the kiss of Nestor (*Troilus and Cressida*, IV, 5).

Beside the life of one of these beings, almost all other characters that ever lived seem but

> As is the morn-dew on the myrtle leafe
> To his grand sea.
>
> (*Antony and Cleopatra*, III, 10)

---

[1] Plato, quoted by Burton, *The Anatomy of Melancholy.*

Their griefs, their joys, are vast as those of the elements, of the universe, of the heavens.

> Will Caesar weepe ?
>> He has a cloud in's face.
>>> (*Antony and Cleopatra*, III, 2)

Cleopatra's ' passions are made of nothing but the finest part of pure love. We cannot call her winds and waters sighes and teares ; they are greater stormes and tempests than Almanackes can report. This cannot be cunning in her ; if it be, she makes a showre of rain as well as Jove' (*Antony and Cleopatra*, I, 2).

The passions of these beings are great and irresistible as the rising of the sap in spring — as in the wild and unlawful springtime love of these lines :

PANDARUS : . . . he will weepe you, an 'twere a man borne in Aprill.

CRESSIDA : And Ile spring up in his teares, an 'twere a nettle against May.   (*Troilus and Cressida*, I, 2)

Iras, looking at the hand of her fellow waiting-woman, Charmian, says :

> There's a Palme presages Chastity, if nothing else,

Charmian replies :

> E'ne as the ore-flowing Nylus presageth Famine.
>> (*Antony and Cleopatra*, I, 2)

And we see the veins of the hand changed to long rivers in that fruitful earth.

A narrow bed is changed to the Indies with all its splendours :

> Her bed is India ; there she lyes, a Pearle :
> Betweene our Ilium and where she resides
> Let it be cald the wild and wandring flood,
> Ourselfe the merchant, and this sayling Pandar
> Our doubtfull hope, our envoy and our Barke.
>> (*Troilus and Cressida*, I, 1)

It is great morning,

So said Paris in the opening of the Third Scene of the Fourth Act of *Troilus and Cressida*. And, by the light of that great morning, even the beings whom we see passing in the common street are transformed for us, for evermore, into the epitome of all beauty, or all sorrow. We ask

Who were those went by ?   (I, 2)

and the answer comes :

Queen Hecuba and Helen.

.   .   .   .

In the Tragedies the themes are these : the struggle of Man against the gigantic forces of Nature, or of Man brought face to face with the eternal truths. . . . The King made equal with the beggar at the feast of the worm, the King whose will had never been combated, finding that his hand ' smelles of mortalitie '. The King who

Strives in his little world of Man to outscorne
The to-and-fro conflicting wind and rain.
                    (*King Lear*, III, 1)

(When the rain came to wet me once and the wind to make me chatter, when the Thunder would not peace at my bidding, there I found 'em, there I smelt 'em out. Go to, they are not men o' their words : they told me, I was everything : 'tis a Lie : I am not Agu-proofe.)
                    (*King Lear*, IV, 6)

Macbeth and Lady Macbeth, hunted through the days and nights by the Furies their crime has summoned from the depths of their own souls — those Furies who drag down the days and nights upon them, until light is as darkness, darkness as light :

MACBETH : What is the night ?
LADY MACBETH : Almost at odds with morning, which is which.

Death quenching the light of beauty and of youth, quenching love :

> The jawes of darknesse do devoure it up :
> So quick bright things come to confusion.

Timon of Athens digging with his nails in the wilderness to unearth the most humble root wherewith to appease his hunger, and finding, at first, not a root, but uneatable gold, the source of all evil. The world of Hamlet, that ' distracted globe ' that holds his brain, ruled over by a small star.

These are the themes. The night of King Lear would seem to blot out all life. Here the great creator of these Hymns to Life has given us a work that is largely a diatribe against procreation — uttered, perhaps, at a time when darkness had engulfed his own soul.

Yet even here, Lear, cursing his daughter, Goneril, calls upon Nature to

> Dry up in her the organs of increase

as the most appalling curse that may fall.

And here, as throughout the Tragedies, Man may rise to such a height that he can speak, as an equal, with Fate, although he is in her power :

KENT : Fortune, good night, smile once more, turn thy wheel!

Man speaks with the gods, though the answer of the gods sounds through strange mouths . . . the voice of the Oracle speaks through the lips of three passers-by in the market-place :

> ' 'Tis verie like he hath the Falling sicknesse.'
> ' No, Caesar hath it not ; but you and I
> And honest Casca, we have the Falling sicknesse.'
> ' I know not what you meane by that, but I am sure Caesar fell downe. If the rag-tagge people did not clap him and hisse him, according as he pleas'd and displeas'd them, as they use to do the players in the theatre, I am no true man.'
> *(Julius Caesar, I, 2)*

But those passers-by, through whose lips the Oracle spoke, were to be the murderers of Caesar.

The voice of Fate sounds through the lips of Macbeth's porter. As the knocking on the Castle gate changes to the noise of the Damned knocking at the gate of Hell, so that voice changes to that of the porter at Hell's gate.—The Castle is no longer the Castle, but the place of the Damned, of that ' Farmer that hang'd himselfe on th' expectation of Plentie ' — (the woman to whom the harvest was of the physical world, — who sowed, who reaped, and who, in the end, hanged herself when the reaping was done, and she knew the worth of the harvest) — and the man ' who committed Treason enough for God's sake, yet could not equivocate to Heaven : O, come in, Equivocator '.

Throughout the Tragedies there are strange mutterings, as of a sibyl prophesying Doom :

> '. . . There was such laughing.   Queen Hecuba laught that her eyes ran Ore.'
> '. . . with millstones.'
> ' And Cassandra laught.'
>
> (*Troilus and Cressida*, I, 2)

Or a ghost turns prophet :

BRUTUS :   Why comst thou ?
GHOST :   To tell thee thou shalt see me at Philippi.
BRUTUS :   Well, then I shall see thee againe ?
GHOST :   I, at Philippi.
BRUTUS :   Why, I will see thee at Philippi then.

> (*Julius Caesar*, IV, 3)

And from the lips of another ghost sounds this prophecy :

> And duller shouldst thou be than the fat weede
> That roots itself in ease on Lethe Wharfe,
>
> (*Hamlet*, I, 5)

.   .   .   .   .   .

The beating of these greater hearts, the pulse of this vaster humanity, seem energised by the rhythms, which are like the ' active principles ' of which Newton wrote.

Shakespeare's immense benevolence and love, and the

C

dooms which are shadows cast by these huge characters —
(shadows bearing their shape, moving in accordance with
their movements) — are conveyed through the world of
sound. Through rhythm, which is 'the mind of dance
and the skeleton of tone', and through tone, 'which is the
heart of man', 'this organic being clothed with the flesh
of the world'.[1]

At moments in the very sound of the verse or the prose,
is heard the tread of Doom. The beating of Macbeth's
heart changes, suddenly, to the knock of Fate's hand upon
the door, in the passage quoted above, where the Porter
hears the Damned knocking at the gate of Hell.

PORTER : Here's a knocking indeede ! If a man were Porter of
Hell-gate he should have olde turning the key. Knock,
knock, knock . . . But this place is too cold for Hell.

And why is it too cold for Hell ? Because of the coldness of the will that planned the deed ? Because the upper
circles of Hell are warmed by some human passion, and
the Porter knew nothing, as yet, of the utter darkness ? Or
was it, not the tread of Doom, the knocking of the damned
souls, that was heard, but (as Sir Arthur Quiller-Couch
suggested, in *Shakespeare's Workmanship*) 'the sane, clear,
broad, ordinary workaday world asserting itself, and none
the more relentingly for being workaday, and common and
ordinary, and broad, clear, and sane ' ?

.   .   .   .   .   .

And what of Shakespeare's ' tuneful plannetting ' ? [2]
If we consider the celestial and terrestrial mechanics of
Shakespeare's vast music, at times the movement of the
lines is like that slow astronomic rhythm by which the
northern and southern atmospheres are alternately subject
to greater extremes of temperature. So it is, I think, with
Othello. Sometimes the verse is frozen into an eternal polar

[1] Richard Wagner, *Opera and Drama*.
[2] Leigh Hunt's description of poetry.

night, as in certain passages of *Macbeth*. Sometimes it is like the sun's heat, as in *Antony and Cleopatra* ; sometimes it is the still-retained heat of the earth, as in *King Henry the Fourth* and *King Henry the Fifth* (works of a very different order from that of the Tragedies). It moves like Saturn in the Dorian mode, like Jupiter in the Phrygian.

Sometimes the gigantic phrases, thrown up by passion, have the character of those geological phenomena, brought about in the lapse of cosmical time, by the sun's heat, by the retained internal heat of the earth, — or they seem part of the earth, fulgurites, rocky substances fused or vitrified by lightning, as in *Timon of Athens*. Or, as in *King Lear*, the words seem thunderbolts, hurled from the heart of heaven. *King Lear*, *Timon of Athens*, seem the works of a god who is compact of earth and fire, of whom it might be said that he is a fifth element.

The immense differences in shape and character between the caesuras in his verse, and between the pauses that end the lines, have much to do with the variation of sound, rhythm, and movement.

Sometimes the pause is like a whirlpool or vortex, as in the first line of Othello's

> Excellent wretch ! Perdition catch my Soule,
> But I do love thee. And when I love thee not,
> Chaos is come againe.

Here, between ' wretch ' and ' perdition ', the caesura has a swirling movement. But the most wonderful of all uses of the caesura occurs in *Macbeth*, as we shall see.

V

'MACBETH'

THE events in the life of a character, as well as the personality, even the appearance of Shakespeare's men and women, are suggested by the texture, the movement of the lines. In *Macbeth*, for instance, we find, over and over again, schemes of tuneless dropping dissonances :

FIRST WITCH

When shall we three meet againe ?
In thunder, lightning, or in raine ?

SECOND WITCH

When the hurly-burly's done,
When the battle's lost and won.

THIRD WITCH

That will be ere set of Sun.

FIRST WITCH

Where the place ?

SECOND WITCH

Upon the heath.

THIRD WITCH

There to meet with Macbeth (I, 1).

'Done' is a dropping dissonance to 'raine', 'heath' to the second syllable of 'Macbeth', and these untuned, dropping dissonances, falling from the mouths of the three Fates degraded into the shapes of filthy hags, have a prophetic and terrible significance.—So do Macbeth and Lady Macbeth, slow step by step, descend into Hell.[1]

---

[1] 'When the battle's lost and won . . .' Could anything be more significant of the absolute stony indifference of the three hags, — seeing all things alike, seeing evil in all things ?

Charles Lamb said of these witches: '. . . The hags . . . have neither child of their own, nor seem to be descended from any parent. They are foul anomalies, of whom we know not whence they are sprung, nor whether they have beginning or ending. . . . Except Hecate, they have no names — which heightens their mysteriousness.'

Has not Macbeth himself brought them into being ? . . . The first speech of these three Fates ends thus :

> Fair is foul, and foul is fair :
> Hover through the fog and filthy air.

The first words spoken by Macbeth are, as Bradley has pointed out, nearly an echo of this :

> So foul and fair a day I have not seen.

But that great critic omitted to call attention to the fact that sometimes the Apparitions' voices sound with the very tone of Lady Macbeth's voice :

> Be bloody, bold, and resolute.

Might this not have come from the lips of Macbeth's loving Fury ? And does not Lady Macbeth, herself, apostrophising her absent husband, say :

> Hie thee hither,
> That I may pour my spirits in thine ear.

Here, as is usual with Shakespeare, a phrase does not bear its obvious meaning alone.

Sir Arthur Quiller-Couch has said ' the whole play, as it were a dark corridor of Inverness Castle, resounds with . . . echoes '.

These echoes fall because Time (as has been pointed out by two distinguished poets and critics,[1] working independently and from quite different points of view) ' has become inoperative ', no longer means anything. Mr. Stephen Spender says :

[1] Mr. Stephen Spender and Mr. Mark van Doren.

'One often hears quoted :

> Come what may
> Time and the hour run through the roughest day.

Actually, the tragedy of Macbeth is in his discovery that this is untrue.

. . . .

'In the minds of Macbeth and Lady Macbeth there are, after the prophetic meeting with the weird sisters, three kinds of time : the time before the murder of Macbeth, the time of the murder of Duncan, and the enjoyable time afterwards, when they reap the fruits of the murder. Their problem is to keep these times separate, and not to allow them to affect each other.'

Quoting Macbeth's soliloquy before the murder,

> If it were done — when 'tis done — then 'twere well
> It were done quickly : if the assassination
> Could trammel up the consequence, and catch
> With his surcease, success : that but this blow
> Might be the be-all and the end-all here,
> But here upon this bank and shoal of time
> We'ld jump the life to come. But in these Cases
> We still have judgement here : that we but teach
> Bloody instructions, which, being taught, return
> To plague the inventor (I, 7).

Mr. Spender remarks : 'Macbeth certainly has good reason to fear even-handed justice. . . .

'The real fear is far more terrible. It is a fear of the extension into infinity of the instant in which he commits the murder. The bank and shoal of time is time that has stood still ; beyond it lies the abyss of a timeless moment.'

Later, Mr. Spender refers to Lady Macbeth's

> . . . Nor time, nor place,
> Did then adhere, and yet you would make both.
> They have made themselves, and that their fitness now
> Does unmake you (I, 7).

In this, I see that Time and Place have become active principles, — a part of Destiny.

This illuminated criticism explains, of course, both Lady Macbeth's insistence on the hour in the sleep-walking scene, and the repetition in a speech of Macbeth's — the perpetual return to :

> Shall sleepe no more.

The words of Banquo to the witches :

> If you can look into the seeds of Time,
> And say which grains will grow and which will not,

' plant early in the play ', says Mr. van Doren,[1] ' a conception of time as something which fulfils itself by growing — and which, the season being wrong, can swell to monstrous shape. Or it can find crannies in the mold, and extend secret sinister roots into dark soil that never has known them. Or it can have no growth at all, and rot and fester in its bed and die. The conception wavers, like the courage of Macbeth, but it will not away. Duncan welcomes Macbeth to Forres with the words :

> I have begun to plant thee, and will labour
> To make thee full of growing.

' But Macbeth like Time itself, will burgeon beyond all bounds.'

I think it means this — but has, also, another meaning. We plant our death in the man who will be the means of it. Not only his deformity, but the looks and taunts of his fellow men planted evil in the nature of Richard the Third. As for Edmund — such speeches as that made by his father to Kent were responsible for his nature.

Perhaps the good Duncan had planted ambition — which was to be the cause of his own death — in Macbeth.

In this vast world torn from the universe of night, there

[1] Mark van Doren, *The Plays of Shakespeare*.

are three tragic themes.   The first theme is that of the actual
guilt, and the separation in damnation of the two characters
— the man who, in spite of his guilt, walks the road of the
spirit, and who loves the light that has forsaken him — and
the woman who, after her invocation to the ' Spirits who
tend on mortall thoughts ', walks in the material world, and
who does not know that light exists, until she is nearing
her end and must seek the comfort of one small taper to
illumine all the murkiness of Hell.—That small taper is
her soul.

There beings have the force, the vastness of Nature.

Dr. Caroline Spurgeon has already, in her book *Imagery
of Shakespeare's Characters*, called attention to ' the *unnatural-
ness* of Macbeth's crime' being like ' a convulsion of
nature '.   This, she says, ' is brought out repeatedly and
emphasised by imagery, as are also the terrible results of
going against nature '.   Macbeth says that Duncan's wounds

> . . . look'd like a breach in nature,
> For ruin's wasteful entrance.

Again, the doomed Queen's malady is ' a great perturba-
tion in nature '.

This, I think, has reference to the crime.   But it shows
Macbeth and his Queen, also, as figures of the same vastness
and eternity as Michelangelo's ' Night and Day '.

The second tragic theme of the play is the man's love
for the woman whose damnation is of the earth, who is
unable, until death is near, to conceive of the damnation
of the spirit, and who in her blindness therefore strays
away from him, leaving him for ever in his lonely hell.

The third tragic theme is the woman's despairing love
for the man whose vision she cannot see, and whom she
has helped to drive into damnation.

The very voices of these two damned souls have therefore a different sound.   His voice is like that of some
gigantic being in torment — of a lion with a human soul.

In her speech invoking darkness, the actual sound is so murky and thick that the lines seem impervious to light, and, at times, rusty, as though they had lain in the blood that had been spilt, or in some hell-born dew. There is no escape from what we have done. The past will return to confront us. And that is even shown in the verse. In that invocation there are perpetual echoes, sometimes far removed from each other, sometimes placed close together.

For instance, in the line

> And fill me from the Crowne to the Toe, top-full

' full ' is a darkened dissonance to ' fill ' — and these dissonances, put at opposite ends of the line, — together with the particular placing of the alliterative *f*'s of ' fill ' and ' full ' and the alliterative *t*'s, and the rocking up and down of the dissonantal *o*'s (' Crowne' ,' Toe ', ' top ') show us a mind reeling on the brink of madness, about to topple down into those depths, yet striving to retain its balance.

Let us examine the passage for a moment. The manner in which the stressed assonances are placed is largely responsible for the movement, and the texture is extremely variable — murky always, excepting for those few flares from the fires of Hell, but varying in the thickness of that murk.

> The Raven himselfe is hoarse
> That croakes the fatall entrance of Duncane
> Under my Battlements. Come, you Spirits
> That tend on mortall thoughts! unsex me here,
> And fill me from the Crowne to the Toe, top-full
> Of direst Cruelty! Make thicke my blood ;
> Stop up the accesse and passage to Remorse,
> That no compunctious visitings of Nature
> Shake my fell purpose, nor keepe peace betweene
> The effect and it. Come to my Woman's Brests,
> And take my Milke for Gall, you murthering Ministers,
> Where-ever in your sightlesse substances
> You waite on Nature's Mischiefe. Come, thicke Night,

> And pall thee in the dunnest smoake of Hell,
> That my keene knife see not the Wound it makes,
> Nor Heaven peepe through the Blanket of the darke
> To cry Hold, Hold.

Throughout the whole of this speech, an untuned and terrible effect is produced by these discordant, dissonantal *o*'s, used outwardly and inwardly — ' hoarse ' echoed by ' croakes ' (I am assuming, from the evidence of other words, that the *oa* of ' croakes ' was then pronounced as an assonance to the ' oar ' of ' hoarse ') — these thickening to ' come ', darkening again to ' mortall thoughts ' and then — supreme example — making the line rock up and down, and finally topple over, in

> And fill me from the Crowne to the Toe, top-full.

' Blood ', ' Stop ', ' Remorse ', ' Come ', — each of these dissonantal *o*'s has a different height or depth, a different length or choked shortness.[1]   There is a fabric, too, of dull and rusty vowels, thickened *m*'s, and unshaping *s*'s — (these latter are unshaping because they are placed close together, and so deprive the line of form, to some extent, as in

> Stop up the accesse and passage to Remorse,
> That no compunctious visitings of Nature

or

> Where-ever in your sightlesse substances).

Throughout the passage, the consonants are for ever thickening and then thinning again — perhaps as the will hardens and then, momentarily, dissolves.   In the lines

> That croakes the fatall entrance of Duncane
> Under my Battlements.   Come, you Spirits

' Come ' is a thickened, darkened assonance (almost a dis-

---

[1] Dissonantal: but in the case of ' Stop ' and ' Come ' hardly so; for in the pronunciation of that line the sound of these particular *o*'s was almost identical — only the end ' *p* ' and ' *m* ' distorted them slightly.

sonance) to the ' Dun ' of Duncane and of the first syllable
of ' under '.   And in the line

That no compunctious visitings of Nature

the first syllable of ' compunctious ' is a kind of darkened,
thickened reverberation of the word ' Come ' (darkened or
thickened because what follows throws a shade backward) ;
the second syllable is a thickened echo of the first syllable
of ' Duncane '.

As the giant shuttles of Fate weave, closing and opening,
so do the lines of this speech seem to close and open, and
to change their length.   But this change is in appearance
only, and not real.   By this I mean that there are no extra
syllables to the line.   The apparent change is due to the
lightening and lengthening of the vowel sounds.   For
though, as I have said already, the words are frequently
dull and rusty in this passage, at times they stretch out into
a harsh shriek, which sometimes is sustained, sometimes
broken, — as with the broken echoes ' Raven ', ' fatall '.

There are moments, too, when the line is prolonged for
other reasons than that of the changing vowel-lengths :

And take my Milke for Gall, you murthering Ministers

is an example.   Here, in spite of the fact that all the vowels
are dulled (with the exception of the high *a* of ' take ' and
the *a* of ' gall '), the *l*'s prolong the line slightly, the thick,
muffled reverberations of the alliterative *m*'s, placed so close
together, produce a peculiar effect of dull horror.   In

Stop up the accesse and passage to Remorse

we shall find that instead of the line being slowed (and therefore, in appearance, lengthened) by the *s*'s, the dull assonantal *a*'s, a more powerful factor, when placed close
together actually shorten the line, which, again, is thickened
by the *p*'s ending words that are placed side by side.   The
effect produced in a line by *p*'s *ending* a word, and by *p*'s
beginning a word, is completely different.   A *p* beginning a
word does not necessarily thicken the line.

Sometimes the particular placing of the assonances produces a sound like that of a fevered, uneven pulse, — an
example is the effect brought about by the drumming of
the dull *un . . . om* sounds in the lines

> . . . Duncane
> Under my Battlements. Come.

This terrible drumming sound is heard over and over again
throughout the passage, and is due not only to the placing
of the assonances, but also to the particular placing of
double-syllabled and — (this has a still stronger effect) —
treble-syllabled words and quick-moving, unaccented one-
syllabled words.   In the line

> And fill me from the Crowne to the Toe, top-full

'to the' gives an example of the effect of those quick-
moving, unaccented one-syllabled words :

> That no compunctious visitings of Nature

is an example of the use of three-syllabled words, disturbing,
purposely, the movement of the line.

This march towards Hell is slow, and has a thunderous
darkened pomp.   It is slow, and yet it has but few pauses
(for that march is of her own will, she is driven by that will
as by a Fury) and these pauses are not long, but deep, like
fissures opening down into Hell.   There is, however, a
stretching pause after the word 'Gall'.

In the Second Scene of Act Two, while the sleeping
King is being sent to his death, Lady Macbeth's voice has a
different tone :

> That which hath made them drunke hath made me bold,
> What hath quench'd them hath given me fire.
>   Hearke !
> Peace !
> It was the Owle that shriek'd, the fatall Bell-man,
> Which gives the stern'st good-night.[1]

---

[1] So it is printed in the Oxford edition. The Second Folio has it thus :
> 'Hark ! Peace !'
in one line, instead of two. This seems to me fatal to the splendour of the passage.

Here we actually feel the silence of the night, broken by that long flame of a voice, like a torch held by a Fury before the destruction of a world is begun. That voice, pausing, as it seems, for ever on the long sound of ' Peace ' (a word that has the high doom-haunted tone of the owl's shriek), echoes, in a straight line, down all the corridors of the Dead.

The speeches of Macbeth have a different sound. He, at least, would retreat from the path, if only it were possible. But he is a prisoner, bound for ever to his first hell-born deed, and he must go where his deed drags him.

The dark and terrible voice of Macbeth is not covered by a blood-dewed rust, is not like a black and impenetrable smoke from Hell, or the torch of a Fury — as is the voice of the woman who, to him, is Fate. It is hollow like the depths into which he has fallen, it returns ever (though it, too, has discordances) to one note, dark as the Hell through which he walks with that sleepless soul. The sound is ever ' no more '.

> Cawdor
> Shall sleepe no more, Macbeth shall sleepe no more.

Dr. Bradley, in *Shakespearean Tragedy*, calls attention to the three beings in one that must suffer damnation. ' What he [Macbeth] heard was the voice that cried " Macbeth does murder sleepe ", and then, a minute later, with a change of tense, denounced him, as if his three names gave him three personalities to suffer in the doom of sleeplessness :

> Glamis hath murder'd Sleepe, and therefore Cawdor
> Shall sleepe no more, Macbeth shall sleepe no more.

The despair of Macbeth, hearing the voice that cries these words, his sense that there is no escape, is brought home to us by the dark, hollow, ever-recurrent echoes of the *ore . . . aw* sounds. That is the keynote of the whole speech.

As with Lady Macbeth's speech quoted above, the

magnificence is largely brought about and controlled by the particular places in which the alliterations and assonances are placed (though in the two speeches they are used completely differently, and have an entirely different effect).

MACBETH

Me thought I heard a voyce cry ' Sleepe no more ',
Macbeth does murder Sleepe, the innocent Sleepe,
Sleepe that knits up the ravell'd sleave of Care,
The death of each daye's Life ; sore Labour's Bath,
Balme of hurte mindes, Great Nature's second Course,
Chiefe Nourisher in Life's Feast——

LADY MACBETH
                         What doe you meane ?

MACBETH

Still it cry'd ' Sleepe no More ' ! to all the house :
Glamis hath murder'd Sleepe, and therefore Cawdor
Shall sleepe no more, Macbeth shall sleepe no more.

The hollow vowels are like ' Burrows, and Channels, and Clefts, and Caverns, that never had the comfort of one beam of light since the great fall of the Earth '.[1]

Twice, a word shudders in that dark voice. The first time, it is the word ' innocent ' — that word which must henceforth fly in terror from the voice that uttered it, — but that will yet sound again from those guilty lips, bringing with it a renewed agony of soul.

Sometimes an awe-inspiring, drum-beating sound is heard. Once it is slow, and is caused by placing alliterative *b*'s, with near-assonantal vowel-sounds — ' Bath ', ' Balme ' — (these being pronounced at that time ' Bawth ', ' Baulme ') — at the end of one line and the beginning of the next. (There is a strong pause between these words.) These dark *a*'s are not an exact assonance, because of the difference in thickness between the *th* and the ' *lme* '. Then, for a second time, two *a* sounds are placed together, ' Great

---

[1] Burnet, *The Theory of the Earth.*

Nature's ', and here the beat is less emphatic; there is no pause between the sounds.

But above all, the quickened beat of a terror-stricken heart is heard, in ' therefore Cawdor ' — ' fore ' being a darkened dissonance to ' there ', and the two other syllables being as nearly as possible assonances to ' fore ', to ' Balme ' and to ' Bath ', though all have different degrees of darkness.

This is followed by the long, stately, and inexorable march of Doom :

> Shall sleepe no more, Macbeth shall sleepe no more.

It is in this scene that we first become aware of the different paths of damnation, — the path of the spirit that sees not all great Neptune's ocean will wash his hand clear of blood, — and that of the earth-bound Fate who, until she is near her end, dreams that

> A little water cleares us of this deede,

and who, when the voice cries

> Cawdor
> Shall sleepe no more, Macbeth shall sleepe no more.

hears only the small voice of the cricket — or a dark, but yet human voice :

MACBETH

I have done the deed. Didst thou not heare a noyse ?

LADY MACBETH

I heard the Owle screame, and the Crickets cry.
Did not you speake ?

MACBETH

When ?

LADY MACBETH

Now.

MACBETH

As I descended ?

LADY MACBETH

Aye.

MACBETH

Hearke !
Who lyes i' the second chamber ?

LADY MACBETH

Donalbaine.

.   .   .   .

' Did not you speake ? . . .' Often, in this drama, Fate takes to herself, and uses, the voice of one of the protagonists. . . . And, as Macbeth must hear the voices of the three Sisters and the Apparitions speaking through the lips of his wife, and her voice through theirs — (' Be bloody, bold, and resolute '. Who spoke those words : ' who was it thus that cry'd ? ' as Lady Macbeth asked) — so, here, in the words ' As I descended ', it may be that the descent was into Hell, and that his doom spoke through his unknowing lips.

Doom and he were one.

Macduff, discovering the murder of the King, shouts :

> Banquo and Donalbain ! Malcolm ! Awake !
> Shake off this downy sleepe, Death's counterfeit,
> And looke on Death itselfe ! — up, up, and see
> The great Doome's image ! — Malcolm ! Banquo !
> As from your graves rise up, and walk like sprights
> To countenance this horror ! (II, 3).

These words, that have a strange echoing sound like that of a boulder being thrown into deep water, must have struck the soul of the guilty man with terror.

. . . Malcolm, who must fly, if he would escape his father's fate, Banquo, who must soon die, are called as from their graves, — and to look on what ? The great Doome's image. Duncan ? *Or Macbeth*. For so he must have seen himself — as the great Doome.

Before the first murder was accomplished, the act that

was to be done had slain the half of Nature, — in the world, and in the hearts of Macbeth and Lady Macbeth :

> Now o'er the one-halfe world
> Nature seemes dead. . . .

So the innocent Night and its peacefulness seemed to Macbeth. As Johnson says : ' over our hemisphere all action and motion seem to have ceased '.

From now onward, only blood, and the road that he must tread, exist for Macbeth in the tangible world.

> Who lyes i' the second chamber ?

. . . Who must be the next to fall under his blood-stained hands, upon that road ? . . . But to Lady Macbeth, he is speaking, not of a grave that must be dug, and of a man about to die, but of one sleeping in his bed — Donalbain.

Here, then, in these few lines, the two guilt-stricken souls say farewell, for ever. The immense pause after Lady Macbeth's ' Aye ' is a gap in time, like the immense gap between the Ice Age and the Stone Age, wherein, as Science tells us, ' the previously existing inhabitants of the earth were almost wholly destroyed, and a different class of inhabitants created '. — On the other side of that gap in time, Macbeth rises as the new inhabitant of a changed world — and alone in the universe of eternal night, although the voice of Lady Macbeth, his Fate, his loving Fury, still drives him onward.

Here we have one stupendous use of the pause. After the words that follow Lady Macbeth's ' Donalbaine ', Macbeth looks at his hands.

MACBETH

This is a sorry sight.

The four beats falling upon the silence before Macbeth speaks thus, seem like the sound of blood dropping, slowly, from those hands —

> What hands are here ! Hah ! they plucke out mine Eyes.

D

Those hands are the hands of Murder. They are no longer the hands of the living man who was once Macbeth — hands made to caress with, hands made to open windows on to the sun and air, hands made to lift the life-giving food to the mouth. Those hands have now given him darkness for ever — a darkness surrounded by a terrible and all-seeing light, that mars every action, and that yet has no part in him.

'Io venni in luogo d' ogni luce muto.'[1]

And yet these beings, and those who surround them, speak ever of the light.

How may the sun have appeared to them ? Seeming, at noon, 'as blank as a clouded moon', and shedding 'a rust-coloured ferruginous light on the ground and the floors of rooms',[2] as at a time of earthquake ? — Surely, to them, the sun must often hide his head, or appear 'with a discoloured face, pale like so many ghosts, with a dusty or bloody countenance', or, 'as in some foggy days, hang in the firmament like a lump of blood'.[3]

Though these souls are separated for ever, yet sometimes the appalling necessities arising from their crime leash them together for a moment . . . as in the scene (Act III, Scene 1) where, with a sort of crouching, horror-inspiring quietness, like that of a tiger about to lap blood, Macbeth says

Heere's our chiefe Guest.

And, stretching beyond him, straining even more eagerly towards the doomed Banquo, Lady Macbeth continues :

If he had beene forgotten,
It had beene as a gap in our great Feast
And all-thing unbecomming.

[1] 'I came into a place of all light dumb.'
[2] Gilbert White, *The Natural History of Selborne.*
[3] *Et seq., Theory of the Earth.* Burnet, *Concerning the Conflagration.*

— the sound of the word 'forgotten' being like that of a beast lapping.

Macbeth then says :

> To-night we hold a solemne Supper, sir,
> And Ile request your presence.

(Here, as always, drawing down his own doom upon himself.)

Banquo murmurs :

> . . . Let your Highness
> Command upon me ; to the which, my duties
> Are with a most indissoluble tye
> For ever knit.

. . . That tie is the shedding of his own blood. From the moment of his death he is indeed knit to Macbeth, — he is a part of his Hell.

So did Iago say to Othello :

> I am your owne for ever.

But here, the victim is speaking to the slayer.

A moment later, he says :

> I must become a borrower of the Night
> For a darke houre or twaine.

and Macbeth replies :

> Faile not our Feast.

Says the man who is already half ghost — the ghost who is still a man :

> My lord, I will not.

And Macbeth bids him :

> Adieu, till you returne at Night.

The invited guest was faithful to his promise. The night he must borrow could not hide him long from sight.

Once, and once only, from the lips of the man who

would sleep no more, sounds a voice so stilled, so drowsy, so furred, that it would seem the Conscience itself had begun to fall into an animal slumber.

> There's comfort yet ; they are assaileable ;
> Then be thou jocund. Ere the Bat hath flowne
> His cloyster'd flight, ere to black Hecate's summons
> The shard-borne Beetle with his drowsie hums
> Hath rung Night's yawning Peale, there shall be done
> A deed of dreadfull note.

LADY MACBETH
> What's to be done ?

MACBETH
> Be innocent of the knowledge, dearest Chuck,
> Till thou applaud the deed. Come, Seeling Night,
> Skarfe up the tender Eye of pittiful Day,
> And with thy bloody and invisible Hand
> Cancell and teare to pieces that great Bond
> Which keepes me pale ! Light thickens, and the Crow
> Makes Wing to the Rookie Wood :
> Good things of Day begin to droope and drowse,
> Whiles Night's black agents to their Prey doe rowse.
> Thou marvell'st at my words : but hold thee still,
> Things bad begun, make strong themselves by ill (III, 2).

'. . . Which keepes me pale ' ? . . . What, exactly, does he mean ? Pale from the horror of his own deed ? Or does he mean that he is not yet reddened once more by freshly spilt blood ?

In this passage, the words ' innocent ', ' invisible ', ' pittiful ', shudder as if the guilty man's voice hardly dared utter them. Here, although the sounds of

> Makes Wing to the Rookie Wood :
> Good things of Day

seem huddling together as if for comfort — the discordances, the reversals of ' summons ', ' hums ', ' done ', ' Hand ', ' Bond ', all show that his soul is falling into the frightful pattern of his new life, — that this life has begun to take shape . . . the settling of the pattern is like the cooling of a dead sun.

When we come to the scene where the ghost of Banquo keeps his tryst, we shall hear again the terror-maddened drum-beat of Macbeth's heart :

MACBETH

Avaunt! and quit my sight ! let the earth hide thee :
Thy bones are marrowlesse, thy blood is cold :
Thou hast no speculation in those eyes
Which thou dost glare with.

LADY MACBETH

            Thinke of this, good Peeres,
But as a thing of Custome : 'tis no other,
Only it spoyles the pleasure of the time.

MACBETH

What man dare, I dare :
Approach thou like the rugged Russian Beare,
The arm'd Rhinoceros, or the Hircan Tiger,
Take any shape but that, and my firm Nerves
Shall never tremble. Or be alive againe,
And dare me to the Desart with thy Sword,
— If trembling I inhabit then, protest me
The Baby of a Girle. Hence, horrible shadow,
Vnreall mockery, hence !
               Why so, being gone
I am a man againe. Pray you, sit still.[1]

---

[1] ' If trembling I inhabit then, protest me.'
It is a moot point whether the line should run thus, or whether it should be
          ' If trembling I inhabit thee, protest me.'
Pope changed it to the latter. 'Inhabit' may have seemed to him vague, though it has been used by Shakespeare, elsewhere, in the meaning of ' staying indoors ', without a noun attached : as, in *As You Like It* : ' O knowledge ill-inhabited ! Worse than Jove in a thatched house.' (In this sense, it means ' lodged '.) This has been pointed out by Steevens.
On the other hand, ' inhibited ' has been used by Shakespeare, in the exact sense in which it is used in the debatable line :
        ' A practiser of arts inhibited '   (*Hamlet*).
To ' inhibit ' is to forbid.
    The original reading is
        ' If trembling I inhabit, then protest me ',
and my own feeling is that, in changing it, the eighteenth-century precise mind of

In these lines, the terror-stricken heart-beat is produced, as before, by the varying use of alliteration of assonances and near-assonances placed close together within the lines : ' firm ', ' Nerves ', ' never tremble ', ' rugged Russian ', ' Take any shape '. The feeling of unendurably tautened, sharpened nerves is produced by the particular use of vowels that are tuned just above the pitch of almost identical vowels in the preceding word : ' Hircan Tiger ', for instance. The change from ' firm Nerves ' to the higher discordances of ' Hircan Tiger ' is another example. ' Sight ' is a rising dissonance to ' quit ', — rising as terror rises. ' Hide ' is an assonance to ' sight ' but is longer because of the *d*. Further on in the passage there are the dissonances ' Girle ', ' Unrealle ' — (the latter being, as it were, a crumbling shadow of the sound of ' Girle ') — and the rising dissonances ' gone ', ' againe '. All these general discordances add to the impression of a nature alternately sharpened and untuned by fear.

Internally and externally in these lines, there are far-separated, but still insistent, echoes, and these help in part to keep the slow sound together. (' Glare ', ' dare ', ' Beare ', and Lady Macbeth's lower ' Peeres '.)

In the last line :

I am a man againe. Pray you, sit still.

the doom-haunted man has lost even the sound of his own heart-beat. There is no pulse to be heard. There is practically no shape in that line, excepting that given by the caesura, which in this case is a chasm dividing the line. . . .

one of the greatest of all technicians in poetry (and one to whom we owe emendations in Shakespeare of the greatest beauty, and the most subtle beauty) has, for once, won the battle over his ear.

If we say

' If trembling I inhibit thee, protest me '

the line shambles, because of the rhyming ' thee ' and ' me ' being so close together, but unevenly in the line. The deadly pomp of the march through Macbeth's lonely desert is destroyed, and the sense that comes through sound. This is how it appears to me ; but I may be wrong.

For it seems as if all the blood had fled from the heart of Macbeth, to join the blood that had been shed. Blood will haunt his spirit for ever, but will leave the veins like that ' most ghastly thing in Nature ', the bed of the ocean from which the ocean has fled.

After this scene, the gulf separating the two beings is impassable. Not only the change of the world in which they live, but the whole depth of the soul, separates them. They are divided in all but love. . . . She will love him for ever : but he has gone beyond love.

This Avarice

(says Macduff)

> Stickes deeper, growes with more pernicious roote
> Than Summer-seeming Lust : and it hath bin
> The Sword of our slain Kings. . . . (IV, 3).

Ambition, Avarice, had no stronger root than love in Macbeth. But now there is no room for her in that Hell.

He asks her

> What is the night ?

and she replies

> Almost at oddes with morning, which is which (III, 5).

Here, I think, Macbeth is asking if the night is blacker for this fresh crime. But Lady Macbeth is speaking of the physical universe.

Macbeth then utters these words :

> How sayst thou, that Macduff denies his person
> At our great bidding ?

He is speaking to the invisible beings who now, with the past and future victims of his guilt, alone inhabit his world. His wife, surprised by the question, replies :

> Did you send to him, Sir ?

And Macbeth, from his polar solitude, answers this being

of another universe, who is separated from him by the whole darkness of her spiritual blindness :

I heare it by the way : but I will send (III, 4).

From that moment, I think that the appearance of Macbeth must have inspired terror, as if he were no longer a mortal man, but one of those giant comets whom Pliny named Crinitas, ' shaggy with bloody locks . . . having the appearance of a fleece surmounted with a kind of crown, — or one that prognosticates high winds and great heat . . . they are also visible in the winter months, and about the South Pole, but they have no rays proceeding from them '.

And Lady Macbeth — how changed is she, in that pitiful scene when she who had cried to ' thicke Night ' to envelop the world and her soul, she who had rejected light, seeks the comfort of one little taper, — the small candle-flame of her soul, to light all the murkiness of Hell. Yet still, in the lonely mutterings of one who must walk through Hell alone, save for the phantom of Macbeth, we hear that indomitable will that pushed him to his doom, rising once more in the vain hope that she may shield and guide him.

There is, in these two beings, the faithfulness of the lion and his mate. It is not their fault that never more can she be his companion.

To speak of this scene from a technical point of view, the extremely interesting theory was propounded by Mr. M. A. Bayfield, in *A Study of Shakespeare's Versification*, that ' Lady Macbeth's speeches, which have always been printed in prose, are really verse, and very fine verse too. The reader ' (he continues) ' will see how enormously they gain by being delivered in measure, and that the lines drawn out in monosyllabic feet are as wonderfully effective as any that Shakespeare wrote.

' But for the retention of the iambic scheme, the recognition would doubtless have been made long ago, but editors recognise no monosyllabic foot and would hesitate to produce lines with initial " Trochees ".'

The speeches in the sleep-walking scene, if spoken as verse, have a great majesty : they drag the slow weight of the guilt along as if it were the train of pomp. But they have not the infinite pathos of the speeches when they are in prose, they do not inspire the same pity for this vast being, her gigantic will relaxed by sleep, trying to draw that will together, as she wanders through the scenes of her crime. The more relaxed sound of the prose produces that effect. The beat of the verse should be felt rather than heard, underlying the speeches.

Again, there will come one of those reminiscent whispers — the words of Macbeth when he hears of her death. . . .

> Out, out, brief candle. . . .

And we see again that lonely being, wandering through Hell with the help of one small light. But to Macbeth the weak light of the candle was not to be treasured, as a hope in the midst of the increasing darkness.

Macbeth like that lonely sleep-walker, had changed. That change began when he, alone, heard the voice that cried ' Macbeth has murdered Sleepe ', — and knew that he was alone for ever. He, who, in the midst of the darkness in that universe his soul, could yet love the light, is about to turn from it, for he must undergo the Mesozoic Age, the Age of Stone :

> I gin to be aweary of the Sunne.

And after the piteous human longing of

> Cure her of that.
> Canst thou not Minister to a minde diseas'd,
> Plucke from the Memory a rooted Sorrow,
> Raze out the written troubles of the Braine,
> And with some sweet oblivious Antidote
> Cleanse the stufft bosome of that perilous stuffe
> Which weighs upon the heart ?

the words

> She should have dy'd hereafter ;
> There would have beene a time for such a word :

in their very quietness, their slowness, seem tears shed in
the soul by those lidless eyes, an oblation, the wasting of a
rock or glacier by water-dropping, by melting.

Those two beings have passed even from the darkness
of a world in which it was possible to ask

> Is it Night's predominance, or the Daye's shame,
> That darknesse doth the face of Earth intombe,
> When living Light should kiss it ? (II, 4)

— a darkness of which they have become so much natives
that night and day are one.

MACBETH : What is the night ?
LADY MACBETH : Almost at oddes with morning, which is
   which —

but that yet is illumined by the vision of a lost heaven —
a heaven that lives yet in spite of their fall :

> ' Angels are bright still, though the brightest fell.'

VI

' KING LEAR '

As flies to wanton boyes are wee to the Gods :
They kill us for their sport.

' HERE ', wrote Swinburne, ' is no need of the Eumenides,
children of Night everlasting, for here is very Night herself.
The words just cited are not casual or episodical, they strike
the keynote of the whole poem, lay the keynote of the whole
arch of thought. . . . We have heard much and often from
the theologians of the light of revelation : and some such
thing indeed we find in Æschylus : but the darkness of
revelation is here.

' For in this, the most terrible work of human genius,
it is with the very springs and sources of nature that her
student has set himself to deal. The veil of the temple of
our humanity is rent in twain.'

' To see the true light,' said Meister Eckhart, ' one must
become blind and strip God naked of things.'

Here, in this play in which the cry sounds always ' Poor
Tom's a-cold ! ' (Man going bare to Death, or Man under
' the extremitie of the skies ') unrolls before us the history
of a great King powerful and ancient as the heavens, who
must learn that his hands ' smelle of mortalitie ' — and who,
through the darkness of the mind, reaches the Night of the
Soul (but not that which is known by the Saints) — and,
through the Night of the Soul, reaches the light. And this
history is mirrored by that of the great King's lesser counterpart, his servant Gloucester — the lusts of the heart in
Gloucester taking the place of the pride of the will.[1]

[1] ' What could better point the transcendent issues Shakespeare has developed
. . . than this encounter of the sensual man robbed of his eyes, with the wilful man,
the light of his mind put out.'— GRANVILLE-BARKER, *Prefaces to Shakespeare.*

Cries the mad Lear to his blinded servant :

> O, ho ! are you there with me ? No eyes in your head,
> nor money in your purse. Your eyes are in a heavy case,
> your purse in a light : yet you see how this world goes.
> GLOUCESTER : I see it feelingly.
> LEAR : What ! Art mad ? A man may see how this world goes
> with no eyes (IV, 6).

One of the keynotes of the play, I suggest, is the phrase
spoken by the supposed madman, Edgar :

> . . . Nero is an angler in the lake of Darknesse (III, 6).

In Book II, Chapter 37, of Pausanias' *Description of
Greece* occurs this passage :
' I saw also a spring, called the spring of Amphiaraus,
and the Alcyonian Lake. Through this lake, the Argives
say, Dionysus went to Hell to fetch up Semele ; and they
say that Polymnus showed him the way down to Hell.
The lake is bottomless. I never heard of any one who was
able to sound the depth. Nero himself made the experi-
ment, taking every precaution to ensure success. He had
lines made many furlongs long : these he joined together
and weighted with lead, but he could find no bottom. I
was told, too, that smooth and still as the waters of the lake
look to the eye, it yet has the property of sucking down
any one who is rash enough to swim in it. The water
catches him, and sweeps him down into the depths.'
The meaning of this line of Edgar's, taken in conjunction
with the above passage (to which, I would suggest, it must
refer), is of an appalling greatness and terror.
' The lake of darknesse ' — the bottomless depths of
human nature, in which the mad Lear, the blinded Gloucester
(in that world in which child turns against parent, Nature
against Man), and the ghost of Nero the matricide, find
blackness after blackness, depth beneath depth.
Nor is this all. In many a line of Shakespeare's there
is a second meaning, — and this lake through which

Dionysus went to Hell to fetch up Semele, may also be the
lake of human sorrows through which (in this world of
transpositions) Lear and Gloucester, the fathers, went to
recover the beloved Cordelia, the beloved Edgar.

Higden, as translated by Trevisa, uses this appalling
phrase : '. . . he' (Nero) 'let kerne his own moder wombe,
for he wolde see the place that he was conceyved in '.

And Shakespeare evidently regarded Nero as the pattern
of all matricides.

In *King John* (V, 2) occur the lines :

> Yon bloody Neros, ripping up the wombe
> Of your deere Mother England.

There is a reference to Nero as a matricide in *Hamlet*,
and one to his cruelty in the Third Part of *King Henry the
Sixth* (III, 1).

I ask myself, therefore, if the image of Nero angling in
the lake of darknesse may not, in addition to those meanings I have suggested, be an image of Lear, who, in his
prayer to Nature to kill the sources of life in his daughter,
struck at the very heart of Nature, disturbing that lake of
darknesse, the original chaos from which all being arose.[1]

The old King, the events of the play, have the hugeness
of Nature's forces. With the ' waters of old fond eies '

. . . poor old heart, he holp the heavens to raine (III, 7).

Those tears have the mightiness of the heavens in dissolu-
tion, that would ' temper clay ' — the cold clay of the earth,

---

[1] There is a foreshadowing of that lake of darkness that has no bottom, in
Edgar's ' Fathom and half, fathom and half ' (III, 4), a speech not given in the
quartos. Of this line, Steevens says : ' He gives the sign used by those who are
sounding the depths at sea'. And may not some light be cast upon the passage,
— (some light upon the first meaning I have suggested) — by these words spoken
by Isabella about Angelo, in the First Scene of the Third Act of *Measure for
Measure*:
> ' His filth within being cast, he would appeare
> A pond as deepe as hell.'

and of Goneril's and Regan's hearts.   The clay of his own nature.

At one moment, the King who had left humanity to its wickedness, as Lot's wife left Sodom, cast a glance over his shoulder at the abandoned and abandoning — moved by an instance of kindness, a redeeming pity in the heart of Man.

In answer to the words of the Messenger sent by Cordelia,

> You shall have anything.

Lear, the humble, replies :

> No seconds ? All myself ?
> Why this would make a man a man of salt,
> To use his eyes for garden water-pottes,
> Ay, and laying Autumne's dust (IV, 6).

— a man of tears, laying the dust that the fullness of life, the ripeness, has laid upon the heart.

Lear knows, now, that he is Nothing.   But with that knowledge of Nothingness comes Patience.   'Nothing.' 'Patience.'   These two words, and the words ' Good Night ', echo through the play.

At first, powerful and ancient as the heavens, the great King calls upon them, as upon an equal, to avenge him upon his unnatural offspring :

> O heavens,
> If you do love olde men, if your sweet sway
> Allow obedience, if yourselves are old,
> Make it your cause, send downe and take my part ! (II, 4)

And Nature, his mother, having heard the appalling curse he pronounces upon his child :

> Dry up in her the organs of increase,

— seeing in this prayer a crime against her holiest laws, an unnatural abomination, turns the prayer

> All the stor'd vengeances of heaven fall
> On her ingrateful top !

against him, pours ' the extremitie of the Skies ' upon his uncovered head.

' How many Oceans of Water would be necessary to compose this great Ocean, rowling in the Air without bounds or banks ? ' . . . ' Some great violence has been offered to Nature, such as we suppose to have been in the General Deluge when the frame of the Earth was broken.' [1] Certainly there had been some change in Nature, or some violence offered her.

' How else', said Nietzsche, writing of the Œdipus myth, ' could one force Nature to surrender her secrets, but by victoriously opposing her . . . *i.e.* by means of the unnatural. It is this intuition I see imprinted by the awful riddle of the destiny of Œdipus. . . . The man who solves the riddle of Nature . . . that double-constituted Sphinx, must also, as the murderer of his father, the husband of his mother, break the holiest laws of Nature.'

In this play, we see the upheaval of all Nature, the reversal of all histories.

In the beginning of the legend, Cronos devoured his own offspring. In *King Lear*, the brood devours the parent, in whom Age had become Time, and Time a fifth element. In the myth of Œdipus, son of Laius, King of Thebes, the Theban King, having learned from the oracle that he was doomed to die by the hand of his own son, exposed that son upon Mount Cithaeron immediately after his birth, with his hands and feet tied together. Here it is Lear, the father, who having first cast from his bosom his child Cordelia, is then shut from the gates to wander under the ' extremitie of the skies ', as an outcast. The eyes, not feet, of Gloucester, the father of Edmund, and the smaller echo of the great King, are pierced, and he is thrust outside the gates, to wander in blindness.

In the Fourth Scene of the Third Act, when Lear says ' I'll talk with this same learned Theban ', the outcast King

[1] Burnet, *The History of the Earth*.

has reversed his rôle. He is no longer Œdipus, but is the Sphinx, who must ask the great question. . . . And it is the naked man exposed upon the mountains — one more naked even than the questioner, — one who has nothing but his bare humanity, who is now Œdipus the Theban, who can give an answer to the Riddle. No longer does the Sphinx, as in the ancient legend, put an oblique question, to which the answer is : ' This is Man '. Instead, bare and terrible, the question is put. Lear, the Sphinx, asks : ' Is Man no more than this ? '

But in this work of Night, no answer comes from the Naked Man, — no direct answer, only a few meaningless words, like dust from the ruins. But behind that huddle of meaningless words lies the true answer : ' Man is nothing '.

The sounds of the words ' Nothing ' and ' patience ' reverberate through the play.

Almost at the beginning, Lear and his daughter Cordelia reply to each other with this word :

LEAR
Speak.

CORDELIA
Nothing, my lord.

LEAR
Nothing !

CORDELIA
Nothing.

LEAR
Nothing will come of nothing : (I, 1) . . .

There are echoes of this in the Fourth Scene of Act One :

FOOL
Can you make no use of nothing, nuncle ?

LEAR
Why no, boy, nothing can be made out of nothing.

And again :

FOOL

Now thou art an O without a figure. I am better than
thou art now ; I am a Fool, thou art nothing.

This is Man, with his ' lendings ' off, — and before the
light came through darkness, through being blind and
having stripped God naked of things.

Lear says :

No, I will be the patterne of all patience,
I will say nothing (III, 2).

When, in the Second Scene of the First Act, Gloucester,
asking to see the letter Edmund pretends to have received
from his brother, says ' The quality of nothing hath not
such neede to hide it selfe ', — it seems like one of those
strange echoes, or sibylline utterances, which abound in
Shakespeare.

Nothing. Nothingness, — and yet in Shakespeare
there is no waste, no barrenness. All is of some use.

In *Hamlet*, the world of the all-seeing, universal light,
where there is no healing, comforting darkness, but only
the shattering darkness that precedes revelation, — in one
of the most terrible aeon-moments of the play, Hamlet asks :

Dost thou think Alexander looked o' this fashion in the
earth ?

HORATIO : E'en so.

HAMLET : And smelt so ? Pah !

HORATIO : E'en so, my lord.

HAMLET : To what base uses we may return, Horatio ! Why
may not imagination trace the noble dust of Alexander, till
he find it stopping a bung-hole ?

HORATIO : 'Twere to consider too curiously, to consider so.

HAMLET : No, faith, not a jot : but to follow him thither with
modesty enough, and likelihood to lead it ; as thus : Alexander died, Alexander was buried, Alexander returneth into
dust ; the dust is earth ; of earth we make loam, and why
of that loam, whereto he was converted, might they not stop
a beer-barrel ?

E

> Imperious Caesar, dead and turn'd to clay,
> Might stop a hole to keep the wind away :
> O ! that that earth which kept the world in awe,
> Should patch a wall to expel the winter's flaw (V, 1).

All things are put to some use. Is there here *only* despair ? Or is it but contempt for the trappings of glory ? Is there here utter annihilation ?

So, in *King Lear*, as in other of the plays, tears seem, not a barren waste overflow, but a sign of the quickening spirit of redemption. They are a life-giving wonder.

> All you unpublish'd virtues of the earth
> Spring with my tears !

'Be your tears wet ?' Lear asks Cordelia. 'Yes, faith. I pray, weep not.' Yet by those tears, he knows that she lives yet, and is not a phantom returned to him from the grave.

There is a foretelling of the tears of the old humbled King, 'laying Autumn's dust', in these lines spoken by Titus, in *Titus Andronicus* :

> O earth ! I will befriend thee more with raine,
> That shall distill from these two ancient urnes,
> Than youth full Aprill shall with all his showres :
> In sommer's drought Ile drop upon thee still ;
> In winter with warme teares Ile melt thy snow,
> And keepe eternall spring-time on thy face
> So thou refuse to drinke my deare sonne's blood (III, 1).

Even when the growth is an evil one, as from the unlawful springtime tears of Troilus, — still it is life that arises from the tears, and not barrenness.

Through the night of the soul, a terrible wisdom comes to the mad King, and his blind and letter prototype. Gloucester says :

> I have no way, and therefore want no eyes ;
> I stumbled when I saw (IV, 1).

The lust of the eyes, the pride of the heart, are gone.[1]

As I said at the beginning of the book, this play would seem to be largely a diatribe against procreation.

EDGAR

The gods are just, and of our pleasant vices
Make instruments to plague us :
The dark and viteous place where thee he got
Cost him his eies (V, 3).

GLOUCESTER *to* LEAR

Dost thou know me ?

LEAR *to* EYELESS GLOUCESTER

I remember thine eyes well enough. Dost thou
squinny at me ? No, doe thy worst, blind Cupid ;
Ile not love (IV, 6).

LEAR (*crying*)

No, they cannot touch me for coyning :
I am the King himselfe.

— the coining to which he refers is, I think, the procreation of his two elder daughters, that base metal.[2]

The lusts of the heart and of the flesh will not keep the body warm in the face of Death.

FOOL : . . . Now a little fire in a wide field were like an old
Letcher's heart ; a small sparke, all the rest on's body cold.
Look ! (*as Gloucester approaches*) here comes a walking fire !
(III, 4)

Were it not, however, for the baseness of mankind,

---

[1] Here, as elsewhere, we are reminded of certain pages in the *Phaedo Dialogue*.

[2] In support of this theory, I would remind the reader of the following lines from *Measure for Measure* :

ANGELO

Ha ! fie, these filthy vices ! It were as good
To pardon him that hath from nature stolne
A man already made, as to remit
Their sawcie sweetnesse that doe coine heaven's Image
In stamps that are forbid ! 'tis all as easie
Falsely to take away a life true made
As to put mettle in restrained meanes
To make a false one (II, 4).

procreation would seem to be the greater good, and the
giving of life the purpose behind all Nature. And at first,
they seem to be so. As the most appalling of all curses,
Lear calls upon his mother and goddess, Nature, to curse
Goneril with sterility.

> Heare, Nature, heare ! deere Goddesse, heare !
> Suspend thy purpose, if thou didst intend
> To make this Creature fruitefull !
> Into her Wombe convey sterility !
> Dry up in her the Organs of increase,
> And from her derogate body never spring
> A Babe to honor her ! If she must teeme,
> Create her child of Spleene, that it may live
> And be a thwart disnature'd torment to her !
> Let it stampe wrinckles in her brow of youth ;
> With cadent teares fret Channels in her cheekes,
> Turne all her Mother's paines and benefits
> To laughter and contempt : that she may feele
> How sharper than a serpent's tooth it is
> To have a thankless childe ! Away, away ! (I, 4)

(Here, the second and third lines — it must be remembered
that the third line was then pronounced with each syllable
sounding : ' To make this Cre-a-ture fru-ite-full ' have no
pause — move with the slow irresistible power and horror
of a tidal wave. There are pauses of uneven lengths, as if
the earth had been worn into chasms by the retreating flood
of passion. Sometimes, there seems to be an upheaval of
the earth itself, as in the sounds of the words ' sterility ',
' derogate '.)

At one moment of his madness, the voice of Lear, the
great King, pardoning the life of a man who should die for
the sin of adultery, changes to that of Nature herself,
blessing the procreation of all life :

> Thou shalt not dye : dye for Adultery ! No :
> The Wren goes too't, and the small gilded Flye
> Do's letcher in my sight.

Let Copulation thrive : for Gloucester's bastard Son
Was kinder to his father than my Daughters
Got 'tweene the lawfull sheets.
Too't Luxury, pell-mell ! for I lacke Souldiers (IV, 6).

The first part of this speech is beneficent but unseeing, like
the sun whose warmth brings into being the life hidden in
insect's egg, in chrysalis, on a garden wall.

After this, the voice that speaks is no longer that of
Nature alone, but is also, once again, the voice of the King
who may condemn. The two voices are fused into one,
as, in uncaring tones, the true reason for the procreation
of life is divulged : that there may be struggle and
destruction :

For I lacke Souldiers !

This is followed by the Stygian, smirching darkness of
Lear's invective against Woman, the lustful, the life-giving.
This darkness at first has shape, but then crumbles, falls at
last into that Chaos in which the world will end.

It is not without a reason that the vastly formed verse
of the first lines, blessing the procreation of life, gutters
down, gradually, into an unshaped prose, whose very words
seem ' the grosser parts of Chaos falling down toward the
centre of the earth '.[1]

Behold your simpering Dame,
Whose face between her Forkes presageth snow ;
That minces virtue, and does shake the head
To heare of pleasure's name ;
The Fitchew nor the soyled horse goes too't
With a more riotous appetite.
Downe from the waist they are Centaures,
Though Women all above :
But to the Girdle doe the gods inherit,
Beneath is all the fiends'.
There's hell, there's darkness, there is the Sulphurous
pit,

[1] Burnet, *op. cit.*

Burning, scalding, stench, Consumption : Fie, fie,
fie ! pah, pah ! Give me an Ounce of Civet, good
Apothecary, to sweeten my imagination : there's
Money for thee.

GLOUCESTER

O ! let me kisse that hand.

LEAR

Let me wipe it first :
It smelles of Mortality (IV, 6).

.   .   .   .   .   .

' Are not all things generated out of their opposites ? I
mean such things as good and evil, just and unjust. . . .
And I want to show that in all opposites there is, of necessity, a similar alternation. I mean to say, for example, that
anything which becomes great must become greater after
being less.'

Thus spoke Socrates, just before his death ; and the
words were reported in the *Phaedo Dialogue*, which I believe
may possibly have been in Shakespeare's mind at the time
of the creation of certain passages in *King Lear*.

I advance this suggestion with the greatest humility,
since I do not wish to exhibit such a spirit as that of ' the
late Mr. Simpson ', to whom Swinburne paid tribute in
A Study of Shakespeare, as one ' who must have had beyond
all other sane men — most assuredly beyond all other fairly
competent critics — the gift bestowed on him by a malig-
nant fairy, of mistaking assumption for argument and
possibility for proof. He was the very Columbus of mares'
nests ; to the discovery of them, though they lay far beyond
the pillars of Hercules, he would apply all shifts and all
resources possible to an Ultra Baconian process of un-
philosophical induction.'

But it is certain that from Lear (the element of fire, the
will, the pride, the passion, which are the essence of fire)
generated the endless cold of Goneril and Regan. To

become greater, Lear became less. Out of his madness
was born his wisdom.

In the first scene of the play, we see the ancient King
take coldness to his heart, for all his denial :

LEAR
So young, and so untender ?

CORDELIA
So young, my Lord, and true.

LEAR
Let it be so : thy truth then be thy dower :
For, by the sacred radiance of the Sunne,
The mysteries of Hecate and the night,
By all the operations of the Orbes,
From whom we do exist and cease to be,
Here I disclaime all my Paternall care,
Propinquity and property of blood,
And as a stranger to my heart and me,
Hold thee from this for ever. The barbarous Scythian,
Or he that makes his generation messes
To gorge his appetite, shall to my bosome
Be as well-neighbour'd, pitied, and reliev'd
As thou my some-time daughter !

At that moment, he lays his heart bare to the cold. While
shuddering at the barbarous Scythian,

Or he that makes his generation messes

(he that devours those of his own begetting), Lear lays his
heart open to the mercy of the brood that tear and devour
their begetter.

So he moves into the universe of the cold.

When Lear says to his daughter :

Your name, fair Gentlewoman ?

this is as quiet as Death, or as Goneril's death-dealing words.
But the quiet of this sentence of Lear's is like that of a
volcano before an earthquake. Regan's words

I pray you, father, being weake, seeme so,

might be the cry of the Furies in the 9th canto of the
Inferno :

> 'Vegna Medusa, sì 'l farem di smalto.' [1]

For this Fury, too, would petrify Medusa. Stone, herself, she changes all to stone. Even the cry of the Fury is
no more a cry : the cold has frozen it to a whisper.

Her voice seems dying away in the cold, at the end of
each phrase :

> O sir ! you are old ;
> Nature in you stands on the very Verge
> Of her confine : You should be rul'd and led
> By some discretion that discernes your state
> Better than you your selfe. Therefore, I pray you,
> That to our sister you do make returne :
> Say you have wrong'd her, sir (II, 4).

Goneril's answer to Lear's cry :

> How sharper than a Serpent's tooth it is
> To have a thanklesse Childe ! . . .
>
> Never afflict your selfe to know the cause ;
> But let his disposition have that scope
> That dotage gives it (I, 4),

is uncaring as the heavens.

. . . .

In this play, of which the beings are gigantic as phantoms
from Thebes or Cyclopian cities, but yet have tides of blood
beating in their veins, one theme is that of the war between
the ordinary nature and the King-nature, the sacred madness
that is genius ; — the war of the waking workaday world,
the ' world of appearance, with its exceeding distrust of the
Titanic powers of Nature ', against ' the rapture of the
Dionysian state, the annihilation of the ordinary bounds
and limits of existence '.[2]

---

[1] ' Let come Medusa, and change we her to stone.'
[2] Nietzsche, *The Birth of Tragedy*. The phrases have a universal application, and
are not describing King Lear.

At first, Goneril and Regan are not, in their own view, nor from the world's point of view, wicked. Their practical natures, the nature of the waking world, must protect the old mad genius-King against himself and his fires.

Indeed, at one moment, the voice of Regan, the evil daughter, seems that of the discerning Fate that will bring the old man wisdom.

> O ! sir, to wilful men,
> The injuries that they themselves procure
> Must be their schoolmasters (II, 4).

At first, these daughters tell themselves that they are but doing their duty towards their father, and towards the world. The sane workaday world, the world of Appearance, must be protected against him. Economies must be effected, a quiet life ensured. But, with power, their coldness hardens, and the evil takes shape. Of the two sisters, Goneril is the greater, in force, in coldness. The difference between them appears when Regan says of Gloucester :

> Hang him instantly.

The colder, infinitely greater Goneril says :

> Plucke out his eyes (III, 7).

Then Regan, from the low horror of her nature, conceives the idea, more frightful even than that of Goneril :

> Goe thrust him out at gates, and let him smell
> His way to Dover.

Gloucester, the sensual man, is to be reduced to the most animal of the senses . . . that in which Man is most deficient, but which is most powerful in, and makes the greatness of, the Beast.

' I have found ', said Leonardo da Vinci in his *Note-Book*, ' that in the composition of human bodies as compared with the bodies of animals, — the organs of sense are duller and coarser. Thus it is composed of less ingenuous instruments, and of spaces less capacious for receiving the faculties of sense. I have seen in the Lion Tribe, that the sense of smell is connected with the part of the substance of the brain which comes down from the nostrils.'

The blind man is to smell, not feel, his way to Dover. The sense of touch is what separated Man from the beasts, and gave him reason.

Gloucester is to become one of the company of the Lion.

'He' (Shakespeare) 'seems to have been asking himself' (said Bradley) 'whether that which he loathes in man, may not be due to some strange wrenching of the frame of things, through which the lower animal souls have found a lodgement in human forms, and there found, to the horror and confusion of the thinking mind — brains to forge, tongues to speak, and hands to execute, enormities which no mere brute can conceive or execute. He shows us in *King Lear* these terrible forces bursting into monstrous life and flinging themselves upon these human beings who are weak and defenceless, partly from old age, partly because they are human and lack the dreadful energy of the beast.'

'Thou chang'd and self-cover'd thing, for shame', says Albany to Goneril. And constantly Lear refers to the covering of Man. It is as if these beings wished to hide their evil souls, taking upon themselves the covering of the beast.

There are references to the 'detested kite', or to the 'false of heart, light of eare, bloudy of hand; Hog in sloth, Fox in stealth, Wolfe in greedinesse, Dog in madnesse, Lyon in prey'.

And in this world of the cold, thinking of Lear's 'dogge-hearted daughters', we see another circle of Hell, where

> Poscia vid' io mille visi cagnazzi,
> Fatti per freddo; onde mi vien riprezzo,
> E verrà sempre, de' gelate guazzi.[1]

[1] 'There saw I countless visages, alas!
Dog-like with cold, that made me shudder, and still
The shudder comes when frozen pools I pass.'
—Trans. L. Binyon.

There is a passage relating to the transference of the baser souls into the bodies of certain animals, in the *Phaedo Dialogue* :

'SOCRATES : . . . The souls, not of the good, but of the evil . . . are compelled to wander about . . . in payment of the penalty of their former evil way of life ; and they continue to wander until through the craving after the corporeal which never leaves them, they are imprisoned finally in another body. And they may be supposed to find their prisons in the same natures which they had in their former lives.

'. . . Those who had chosen the portion of injustice and tyranny and violence, will pass into wolves, or into hawks and kites ; — whither else can we expect them to go ?' [1] — *Phaedo Dialogue.*

The book, *A Declaration of Egregious Popish Impostures to withdraw Her Majesty's Subjects from their Allegiance*, etc., written by Dr. S. Harsnet (afterwards Archbishop of York) by order of the Privy Council, and printed in 1603, is referred to more than once in the scenes with Edgar the supposed madman. Frateretto, who brought the news about Nero, was one of the devils mentioned in the *Declaration* :

'Frateretto, Fliberdigibet, Hoberdidance, Tocobalto, were four devils of the round or morrice. . . . These four had forty assistants under them, as themselves doe confesse.'—HARSNET, p. 49.

As for

> The prince of darkness is a gentleman
> Modo he's call'd, and Mahu.

we find, in Harsnet, in the deposition of the possessed Richard Mainy :

[1] However, there is also much to suggest that Harsnet's *Declaration* was referred to. For in that work there is a scene in which the Jesuits cast out of the possessed Mainy, the seven deadly sins, in the shape of animals, — Mainy, with each casting-out, acting that particular sin.

' Furthermore it is pretended . . . that there remaineth still in mee the prince of all other devils, whose name should be *Modo*.' (He is referred to, elsewhere, as ' the prince Modo '.) *Mahu* was the chief devil possessing Sarah Williams, and Richard Mainy, in his deposition, says, ' When the said priests had dispatched theire business at Hackney ' (where they had been exorcising Sarah Williams), ' they then returned towards mee, upon pretence to cast the great Prince *Modo*. . . .'

When, in Act II, Scene 4, Lear says of the supposed madman Edgar, ' I'd talke a word with this same learned Theban ' — may not the Theban have been at once Œdipus, son of the King of Thebes, — he who could answer the question of the Sphinx, — and one of those two Thebans who were the last companions of Socrates when, released from his chains, he awaited Death. We read of their conversations with Socrates in the *Phaedo Dialogue* :

' The execution of Socrates having been deferred, Socrates talks with two Thebans, Simmias and Cebes, whom by his enchantments he has attracted from Thebes.'

In the *Dialogue*, after a long discussion about the evils of the body and of the senses and the lusts of the body, and of the vain nature of the clothing of Man, it is asked : ' Have sight and hearing any truth in them ? ' ' He (who) has got rid, as far as he can, of eyes and ears and of the whole body, which he conceives of only as a disturbing element, hindering the soul from the acquisition of truth and knowledge . . . is not this the sort of man who, if any man, is likely to attain to the knowledge of true being ? '

Later, Socrates says to the two Thebans, ' Like children, you are haunted with a fear that when the soul leaves the body, the wind may really blow her away, and scatter her, especially if a man should happen to die in a great storm, and not when the sky is calm.'

To which Cebes answers : ' Then, Socrates, you must argue us out of our fears — and yet, strictly speaking, they are not our fears ; but there is a child within us to whom Death is a sort of hobgoblin : him too we must persuade, not to be afraid when he is alone in the dark.'

In *King Lear*, we have one to whom the darkness of the mind brought a wisdom greater than that of Socrates (one who, like Socrates, is soon to cast off the chains of the body) — enduring the utmost rigours of a storm such as might blow the soul away, speaking of the vain nature of the clothing of man, then comforting one who is alone in the dark through the blindness of the eyes, but who had stumbled when he saw.[1] The great King who has known all splendours, all the richness of life, and their true worth, comforts the destitute — him from whom even the sight of the world has been taken.

> Thou must be patient ; we came crying hither :
> Thou know'st the first time that we smel the ayre
> We waul and cry. I will preache to thee : Marke.
>
> .   .   .   .   .   .
>
> When we are borne, we crie that wee are come
> To this great stage of fooles.

And the young man who has worn the rags and known the nakedness of the beggar, comforts those who must live, speaks of the sweetness of living :

> EDGAR
> O ! our lives' sweetness,
> That we the paine of death would hourely die
> Rather than dye at once — taught me to shift
> Into a madman's ragges, to assume a semblance
> That very dogges disdain'd (V, 3) ;

[1] SOCRATES : And were we not saying, long ago, that the soul when using the body as an instrument of perception, that is to say, when using the sense of sight or hearing or some other sense (for the meaning of perceiving through the body is perceiving through the senses) — were we not saying that the soul too, is then dragged by the body into the region of the changeable, and wanders, and is confused ; the world spins round her, and she is like a drunkard. . . .
GLOUCESTER : I stumbled when I saw.

— or speaks of patience, almost with the tones of the King, since endurance has taught him wisdom :

> . . . Men must endure
> Their going hence, even as their comming hither :
> Ripenesse is all (V, 2).

' Are not all things generated out of their opposites ? ' Patience from madness, the richness of the spirit from the destitution of the body.

An agonized human heart ' cries sleepe to death ' throughout the play. His heart, I think, was the Drum of which Lear speaks when summoning Regan and Cornwall :

> . . . bid them come forthe and heare me,
> Or at their chamber doore Ile beat the Drum
> Till it cry sleepe to death (II, 4),

— for next, he cries,

> O me ! my heart, my rising heart ! But, downe !

It is on our hearts, also, that he beats. Not all the agonies even of Othello can pierce our hearts like those of this old man, with his weeping fond eyes — the great outcast King whose hand ' smells of mortalitie '.

How shall it be explained by what sublime genius this old King, so wilful, so terrible in his passions, is yet so near to our hearts that we would cradle him in our arms like a child ? And cradled he is, for all his greatness, like the child whom we must persuade not to be afraid when he is alone in the dark. So did these few loving beings who remained to him — Kent for instance, and Gloucester, see him :

Gloucester says :

> Come hither, friend, where is the King my master ?

> KENT
> Here, sir ; but trouble him not ; his wits are gone.

> GLOUCESTER
> Good friend, I prithee take him in thy armes.

And later, Kent says :

> . . . I am come
> To bid my King and master aye good night (V, 3) ;

Here the great King is seen once more as a child who must be comforted before the darkness of the night.

Sometimes, all becomes a lullaby :

LEAR : Make no noise, make no noise ; draw the Curtains : so, so, so. We'll goe to supper i' the morning. So, so, so.
FOOL : And Ile go to bed at noon (III, 6).

This has been taken, by some commentators, as referring to the Fool's approaching death. Mr. John Gielgud thinks (and with great kindness allows me to quote him as saying so) that the mystery of the Fool's death is explained by the fact that at the time when the play was first produced, Cordelia and the Fool were in all probability acted by the same boy. The audience, therefore, on hearing of Cordelia's death, would be conscious, also, of the death of Lear's ' poor boy '.

It is a beautiful explanation — that these two heavenly innocences, — the warmth at the old King's heart, should be one and the same in the eyes of the beholders.

It is to be remembered, also, that Lear says :

> *And* my poor Foole is hang'd.

As if he referred, not only to Cordelia, but also to a second being — to his ' poor boy '.

. . . .

After the piteous humility of the moment when the King proclaims himself no higher than a beggar at whom the dogs bark :

> . . . the little dogges and all,
> Trey, Blanch, and Sweet-heart, see they barke at me (III, 6),

and :

> You must bear with me.
> Pray you now, forget and forgive : I am old and foolish.
> (IV, 7)

Although there are moments when he thinks that the mortal wound to his brain was gained in battle, as if he were young and great and still acknowledged to be a King :

> . . . Let me have surgeons :
> I am cut to the braines (IV, 6),

the two beings, Cordelia, from whose sorrows

> All you unpublished virtues of the earth
> Spring with my teares ! (IV, 4)

and the old King whose eyes are

> . . . Garden water-pottes,
> Ay, and laying Autumn's dust,

await the coming darkness.

. . . .

When Lear says :

> Pray you, undoe this Button : thank you, sir (V, 3),

— he is, I think, asking to be released from his outworn life . . . from his ' lendings '. . . . So little a thing, now, is Death to him — only the undoing of a button, then the casting-off of the rags of mortality.

. . . .

That world of night, *King Lear*, contains all degrees of darkness, from the lines spoken by Goneril :

> . . . Where's thy drum !
> France spreads his banners in our noiseless land (IV, 2),

(where, by the use of the word ' noiseless ' we are given a land of night where all the sounds of life are quenched in darkness) — to the advance into a still darker night of

> Childe Rowland to the darke tower came (III, 4),

Both the quartos print this alternative :

> Childe Rowland to the dark *towne* came,

It is not for me to pronounce on the rightness or wrongness of this, when men who are learned have judged it better not to do so. But my instinct (and this, alone, can guide me) tells me that 'towne' may have been in that giant mind, and that certain reasons have led to the change to 'tower'.

If he wrote 'towne', originally, then we know, beyond any doubt, what he meant. The 'dark towne' is Death (and the passage was so understood by Byron). But the reasons for the change may have been these. In the dark *towne* the roofs are low ; our house is our coffin. We are huddled together, are one of a nation, are equal.

If we come to the dark *tower*, we are alone with our soul. The roof is immeasurably high, — as high as heaven. In that eternal solitude there are echoes.

. . . .

Consider the change from the anguish of :

> You doe me wrong to take me out o' the grave :
> Thou art a soule in blisse ; but I am bound
> Upon a wheele of fire, that mine own teares
> Doe scald, like molten lead (IV, 7),

to the gentleness, the consoling and tender darkness of these lines, spoken by one to whom a world-wide ruin has, in the end, taught wisdom and resignation :

> No, no, no, no ! Come let's away to prison ;
> We two alone will sing like Birds i' the Cage :
> When thou dost aske me blessing, Ile kneele downe
> And ask of thee forgivenesse : So we'll live,
> And pray, and sing, and tell old tales, and laugh
> At gilded Butterflies, and heare poore Rogues
> Talke of Court newes, and we'll talke with them too,
> Who loses, and who wins ; who's in, who's out ;
> And take upon's the mystery of things,
> As if we were God's spies : and we'll weare out
> In a wall'd prison, packs and sects of great ones,
> That ebbe and flowe by the moone (V, 3).

F

Here, part of the gentleness, the moving sweetness, is given by the fact that in the double-syllabled and treble-syllabled words, in every case excepting in two (' gilded Butterflies ') every hard consonant there may be is softened by an *s*, — ' prison ', ' blessing ', ' forgivenesse ', ' mystery '.

The passages which come immediately before the death of Cordelia have all this heart-breaking sweetness.   Is there another poet in the world who would have dared the use of that five-time repeated trochee in the line quoted below?

> . . . Thou'lt come no more,
> Never, never, never, never, never (V, 3),

— trochees that with each repetition seem dropping further into darkness.   Is there another poet in the world who could have wrung from the simple repetition of one word, such tears ?

. . . .

The sound of the verse is, now of an unparalleled grandeur, now of an equal sweetness and tenderness.

Consider the raging darkness, the furious whirlwind sweep of the second Scene on the Heath, — those gigantic lines in which Lear defies the whole heaven, cries to it to blot out the world :

> Blow, windes, and cracke your cheeks ! Rage ! Blow !
> You Cataracts and Hyrricanos, spout
> Till you have drench'd our Steeples, drown'd the Cockes !
> You Sulphurous and Thought-executing Fires,
> Vaunt-curriers to Oake-cleaving Thunder-bolts,
> Sindge my white head ! And thou, all-shaking Thunder,
> Strike flat the thicke Rotundity o' the world !
> Cracke Nature's moulds, all germaines spill at once
> That make ingratefull Man (III, 2).

The verse has variety as vast as the theme. The first line is an eight-syllabled one ; then, under the sweep of this enormous rage, stretching from pole to pole, the lines rush forward into decasyllabics and even hendecasyllabics — (and this is not always, though it is sometimes, the result of pretended elision).

The movement is hurled backward and forward. In the first line, for instance, of those strong monosyllables ' Rage ', ' Blow ', the first sweeps onward across the world into infinity, the second is hurled backward.

In ' You Sulphurous and Thought-executing Fires ' the vowel sounds mount, like a rising fury, then the word ' Fires ' (with its almost, but not quite, double-syllabled sound) gives again, though with a different movement, the effect of stretching across the firmament.

Part of the immensity of this vast primeval passage is due to the fact that in the line

Vaunt-curriers to Oake-cleaving Thunder-bolts,

the only word that does not bear an accent is ' to '. And part, again, is due to the contrast between the stretching one-syllabled words of the first line and the three-syllabled ' Cataracts ' and four-syllabled ' Hyrricanos ' of the second. Added vastness is given by the balance of the high *a* of ' Rage ' and that of ' Hyrricanos ', and by the huge fall from the *a* in this latter word, to that word's last syllable. Variety in this ever-changing world-tempest is given, too, by the long menacing roll, in the midst of those reverberating thunder-claps, the *c*'s and *ck*'s of the whole passage, the roll, gradually increasing in sound, of the first three words in

And thou, all-shaking Thunder,

rising and stretching to the long first syllable of ' shaking ' and then falling from that enormous height to the immense, long, thickened darkness of the word ' Thunder '.

In such lines as Lear's

Detested kite, thou liest !

and

Beat at this gate that let thy folly in (I, 4),

the single-syllabled words take on the hugeness of those
new-made stones that Deucalion and Pyrrha, the Deluge
being over, found and cast behind their backs, — the bones
of their mother Earth, which were broken into pieces in
that great ruin.

Additional Notes

'KING LEAR' AND THE 'PHAEDO DIALOGUE'

Note I. Thomas Taylor's Notes to the 'Phaedo Dialogue'

'ACCORDING to Orpheus, there are four governments : the first, that of Heaven, which Saturn received, cutting off the genitals of his father. After Saturn, Jupiter reigned, who hurled his father into Tartarus.'

The father of Saturn was Cronos. . . . Time. . . . In Lear, Age had become Time, and Time a fifth element. I see the fundamental maiming of the life-springs of the parent in the fate of Lear, — reflected in the diatribes of Lear against procreation.—E. S.

Note II. The 'Phaedo Dialogue'

SOCRATES : Is not Evenus a philosopher ?
SIMMIAS : I think he is.
SOCRATES : Then he, or any man, who has the spirit of philosophy, will be willing to die ; but he will not take his own life, for that is held to be unlawful !

Consider the raging ' Off, off, you lendings ; come, unbutton here ' of the unregenerate Lear (tearing off his clothes being a symbol of his wish to tear, violently, the soul from the body) — and the later, humble, gentle resignation of

Pray you, undo this Button : thank you, sir.

Note III. Lear and the 'learned Theban'

Mr. Edmund Blunden, in *Shakespeare's Significances*, has the following passage :

73

'Lear, from the first is portrayed as a little inclined to remember his school education. His reply to Cordelia's unhappy "Nothing" is exactly a thesis of the old natural philosopher's "An Aliquid producatur et Nihilo?"'

Nothing will come of nothing!

Soon after, with a reference to 'the barbarous Scythian', he appears to have Horace in mind. He breaks into Latin — 'Hysterica passio' — when describing his physical trouble, 'a fit of the mother'; he compares himself to Prometheus with a vulture at his heart.

'. . . Presently he refers to poor Tom as "this philosopher", and propounds to him a question, not solely suitable to the war of elements all round, but familiar among the ancient philosophers: "What is the cause of thunder?" Even in this is involved, not only the academic interest of Lear, his notion of poor Tom and the weather, but some allusion to the clash of hot and cold, of his own ardent love confronted with the marble-hearted ingratitude of his daughters. We proceed. "Riding over four-inched bridges" and other visions raised by poor Tom's autobiography have stirred Lear's recollections of a famous passage. "Modo is he called and Mahu" chances to rhyme with that. The next title he gives poor Tom is "learned Theban" and after a while that is changed to "good Athenian". In short, fascinated by Tom's amazements, Lear is all the time contemplating the position through the First Epistle of the Second Book of Horace, and particularly through those lines:

Ille per extentum funem mihi posse videtur
Ire poeta, meum qui pectus inaniter angit,
Irritat, mulcet, falsis terroribus implet,
Ut magus; et modo me Thebis, modo ponit Athenis.

"That is the poet for me, the man who can walk the whole tight-rope of his art, the man who distresses me with imaginings, who angers, comforts, fills with unreal horror like a wizard, who makes me be at Thebes one minute and the next at Athens."

. . . .

Towards the end of that scene, he reverts to his caprice of quoting Horace, and orders poor Tom to find some other " garments " — he had only a blanket ; " You will say they are Persian attire, but let them be changed ". This witty stroke is fully appreciated if we see that it plays on the last Ode of Horace, Book First, " Persicos odi, puer, apparatus " (" my boy, Persian attire and I don't agree ").'

. . . .

This seems to me to prove, conclusively, that Horace was in Shakespeare's mind : but I hold, also, that so was the *Phaedo Dialogue*. Over and over again, in Shakespeare, are short sentences which hold several vast meanings.

Note IV. ' King Lear ' and the ' Phaedo Dialogue '

SOCRATES : ' Ought the philosopher to care about the pleasures . . . if they ought to be called pleasures, of eating and drinking ? '

' Certainly not,' answered Simmias.

' And what about the pleasures of love — shall he care for them ? '

' By no means.'

' And will he think much of the other ways of indulging the body — for example, the acquisition of costly raiment or sandals, or other adornment of the body ? Instead of caring about them does he not rather despise anything more than nature needs ? '

Compare the last paragraph of this, with Lear's

O ! reason not the need ; our basest Beggars
Are in the poorest thing superfluous :
Allow not Nature more than Nature needs :
Man's life is cheape as Beastes. Thou art a Lady ;
If onely to go warme were gorgeous,
Why, Nature needs not what thou gorgeous wear'st,
Which scarcely keeps thee warm. But, for true need,
You heavens, give me patience. Patience I need ! (II, 4)

As for the worth of ' the pleasures of love ' — that theme resounds through the play.

Note V

SOCRATES : Many a man has been willing to go to the world below, animated by the hope of seeing there an earthly love, a wife or son, and conversing with them. And will he who is a true lover of wisdom, and is strongly persuaded in like manner that only in the world below he can worthily enjoy her, still repine at death ? Will he not depart with joy ?

LEAR
Thou'lt come no more,
Never, never, never, never, never !
Pray you, undoe this Button ! Thanke you, sir.
Doe you see this ? Looke on her, looke, her lips,
Looke there, looke there !

Note VI. Shakespeare and the ' Phaedo Dialogue '

In Sir John Edwin Sandys' Address to the Academy (read May 27, 1914), he said that Roger Bacon (who was born, probably, in 1214) refers to Plato's *Phaedo*, firstly for its witness to immortality, and secondly, for its commendation of detachment from temporal causes. ' In the case of the *Phaedo* ', adds the Lecturer, ' he may easily have used the current Latin translation.'

According to the same authority, Roger Bacon had explained that ' Plato was better known to the Fathers than Aristotle, because Plato had been translated into Latin '.

This is one way in which Shakespeare may have become acquainted with the *Phaedo Dialogue*.—E. S.

Note VII

'. . . Plato was accessible only in Shakespeare's time through the Latin version, namely, the complete works

translated by Ficino, published at Bâle in 1551, or in another
edition of Ficino's version, published at Venice in 1581, in
Colophon, dated 1570, or in the translation by Janus
Cornarias, published at Bâle in 1561.'—J. CHURTON COLLINS.

Note VIII

The Fool's Songs and 'And my poore Foole is hang'd'

In the Fourth Scene of the First Act, the Fool's strange
and apparently meaningless snatches of song concentrate,
in a few words, the story of the King and his servant
Gloucester :

> Mum, mum.
> He that keepes nor crust nor crum,
> Weary of all, shall want some.
> That's a sheal'd Peascod.   (*pointing to Lear*)

and

> The Hedge sparrow fed the Cuckooe so long,
> That it had it head bit off by it young.
> So, out went the Candle, and we were left darkling.

The sanity of Lear, the head that had worn the crown
destroyed, devoured, that the crown might be taken. . . .
The Cuckooe . . . one who should not have been in the
nest — the bastard Edmund . . .

These songs show the fate of both Lear and Gloucester ;
the third song shows, perhaps, in a distorting mirror, the
Fool's own end :

> A Fox, when one has caught her,
> And such a daughter,
> Should sure to the slaughter,
> If my Cap would buy a Halter ;
> So the Foole follows after.

The Fox . . . the fox whom the Spartan youth bore
close to his heart, until his heart was devoured . . . Goneril
or Regan.

The halter was for himself in the end. Or so I understand it. Before, he had said to the King, ' Tarry, and take the Fool with thee '. He may have meant into the darkness.

Note IX

From time to time, in *King Lear*, the symbol of a wheel is used — culminating in Lear's words :

> Thou art a Soule in blisse, but I am bound
> Upon a wheele of fire, that mine owne teares
> Doe scald, like molten lead (IV, 7).

It has been suggested that Lear's reference was to Ixion and his wheel, since the ingratitude of Ixion was the reason for his punishment.

But I believe the wheel, also, to be the Wheel of Being.

Note X

LEAR

> 'Tis a good blocke !
> It were a delicate stratagem to shooe
> A Troope of horse with felt : Ile put it in proofe,
> And when I have stolne upon these Sonnes-in-Lawe,
> Then, kill, kill, kill, kill, kill, kill (IV, 6).

' This " delicate stratagem " had actually been put in practice about fifty years before Shakespeare was born, as we learn from Lord Herbert's *Life of Henry the Eighth*, p. 41. " And now," says that historian, " having feasted the ladies royally for divers dayes, he " (Henry) " departed from Tournay to Lisle (Oct. 13, 1513) whither he was invited by the Lady Margaret, who caused there a juste to be held in an extraordinary manner ; the place being a fore-room raised high from the ground by many steps, and paved with black square stones like marble, while the horses, to prevent sliding, *were shod with felt* or flocks (the Latin words are *feltro sive tormento*): after which the ladies danced all night." '—MALONE.

Then, kill, kill, kill, kill, kill, kill.

' This was formerly the word given in the English army when an onset was made on the enemy. So in *Venus and Adonis*,

> Gives false alarms, suggesteth mutiny,
> And in a peaceful hour doth cry " *kill, kill* ".'
> —MALONE.

This latter gives additional meaning and poignance to Lear's

> I am cut to the braines.

uttered almost immediately after.

VII

SOME NOTES ON 'HAMLET'

I write with the utmost diffidence about the play on which the most profound speculation has been exerted by the greatest scholars.

With this sense of unworthiness upon me, a few notes must suffice.

The primary theme of the play is as old as Spring — although the daemons of the Fertility Ritual have taken upon themselves bodies of flesh, are moved by tides of blood, cast shadows.

Dr. Gilbert Murray, in a work of profound and strange beauty, *Hamlet and Orestes*, speaks of the common element in the stories of Hamlet, Orestes, and the wild winter-raging Fool Amloði, Prince of Jutland. . . .

'What is the common element in all these stories ? . . . It is the world-wide ritual story of the Golden Bough Kings. . . .'

. . . .

Orestes, the madman and King-slayer, takes his place beside Brutus the Fool, who expelled the Tarquins, and Amloði the Fool, who burnt King Feng at his winter feast. The great Greek scholar Usener, some years since, on quite another set of grounds, identified Orestes as a winter god, a slayer of the summer ('Heilige Handlung', in the *Archiv für Religionswissenschaft*, 1904) :

'He is the ally of death and of the dead, he comes suddenly in the dark ; he is mad and raging, like the winter god Maimakles and the storms.'

. . . .

Of Hamlet's prototype in Saxo, Amloði, Dr. Murray says he is ' the son of Horvendillus or Orvandel, an ancient Teutonic god connected with Dawn and the Spring. His wife was Groa, who was said to be the Green Earth ; he slew his enemy Collerus — Colbor the Hooded — or perhaps the Cold, in what Saxo calls " A sweet and spring-green spot in a budding wood ". He was slain by his brother and avenged by his son.'

Quoting Bradley's passage about the 'soft animal nature' of Gertrude . . . 'she loved to be happy like a sheep in the sun, and to do her justice, she liked to see others happy, like more sheep in the sun ', Dr. Murray adds : ' Just the right character for our Mother Earth. For, of course, that is who she is. The Greek stories speak her name openly : Gaia and Rhea are confessed Earth-mothers, Jocasta only a stage less so. One cannot apply disapproval to the annual re-marriages of Mother Earth.'

So much, shortly, of the origins of the play.

' It is we who are Hamlet ', said Coleridge. And this is true ; because, although Hamlet lives in a dream-world, he is more real than any other being in any work made by man.

We live the lonely life of this soul, cut off from the rest of the world by the mask of identity, and (finding true communication impossible) using the mask, and a mask of words, as a protection.

We see every working of the mind, as only the man in whom these workings take place, can know them, — from the ' confus'd Mass of Thoughts tumbling over one another in the Dark, when the Fancy was yet in its first Work, moving the Sleeping Images of Things towards the Light, there to be distinguish'd, and then either chosen or rejected by the Judgment '.[1]

My friend, Mr. J. G. Wilson, suggested to me in conversation that in this play, for the first time, the workings of the Unconscious are shown rising above the horizon. I believe this to be true.

[1] John Dryden.

In Dr. Jung's *The Integration of the Personality*, occurs this passage :

'When John Huss and Wycliffe preached, the age of the Reformation had begun, and nobody knew it. It was there *in potentia*, but no one could see it with the eyes or touch it with the hands, and thus it was not in consciousness. It was still unconscious like a sun below the horizon, of which a savage might say, " there is no sun ".'

So it was with the events in *Hamlet*. They, too, lay below the horizon of Hamlet's mind.

Hamlet is a hunting story — that of a man who is hunting his own soul, or the truth of his own soul, and who never finds it.

Mr. Harold Rosenberg, in a recent essay (' Notes on Identity ', with special reference to the Mixed Philosopher, Soren Kierkegaard, published in *View*, May 1946) said :

' The central intuition of Greek tragedy . . . is, there is one unique fact that each individual anxiously struggles to conceal from himself, and this is the very fact that is the root of his identity.

. . . .

' Tragedy is the wilful exposure of the hidden fact by which the hero is identified. The curtain rises at the moment when the process of revelation begins. A messenger arrives, an encounter takes place, etc. It is the same in *Œdipus Tyrannus*, *Macbeth*, *Hamlet*, *Othello*. The first gesture begins to place the hero's apparent identity in question. . . . Is he King, or murdering parricide ? Glamis, Cawdor, or . . .? Prince or Clown ? Hero or Subman ? *Hamlet* opens with the line " Who's there ? " The first line of *Macbeth* after the witches' prelude is " What bloody man is that ? " [1]

---

[1] 'KING LEAR : Who is it who will tell me what I am ?
        FOOL : Lear's shadow.'
    This is a strange answer. Is the Fool answering Lear direct, saying he is his own shadow — or is the Fool saying that his shadow will tell him what he is ?— E. S.

'The hero is met with the Socratic demand : "Know Thyself". In each instance, Man is also put into question — is *he* a King, or a murderer, a prince or a clown ? '

Neither Hamlet, nor Lear, nor Angelo, nor the light-liver were what they had believed themselves to be.

'They say the Owle was a Baker's Daughter. Lord, wee know what wee are, but know not what wee may be.'

We do not know that hidden part of the identity which will only grow with Time, or from the event.

In the case of Hamlet, the hero finds that he is indeed

the fat weed
That roots itself in ease on Lethe Wharfe (I, 5),

. . . . . .

Who and what is the ghost ?

Hamlet, on seeing him beckon, says :

My fate cries out . . . (I, 4),

and the ghost *is* Hamlet's fate. He would speak only to the appointed vessel. When Francisco cried ' hey, answer me ; stand, and unfold yourself ' — in the opening scene, there was no reply.

But, from the moment when the message was given, the world turns to a ghost for Hamlet. Nothing remains but the ghost, the deed that should be done, and never will be, and himself.

There seems to be a certain connection between *Hamlet* and *Othello*, which comes next, in time, to *Hamlet*; because the otherwise entirely opposed characters of Hamlet and Iago, live *by* the mind, *in* the mind.

There seems to be a connection, also, in one sense, between *King Lear* and *Hamlet*. One theme of *King Lear*, as I have said already, is the war between the ordinary nature and the King-nature, between the sacred madness that is genius, and the world of Appearance.

The King and Queen in *Hamlet* belong to the world of Appearance — crime or no crime. All the beings in

Hamlet, excepting the Prince, and Ophelia who is a Fertility-ghost, live in a waking world of action.

And yet theirs is a world of make-believe. Even the Prince, at moments, finds in it a refuge. But this man who lives by thought alone, half deceived by the faults of his own nature, sees the truth, though at moments he denies it. These ordinary beings, living by the body, see the truth never. Truth shines (or, turned black and terrible, rages) round them, over them, under them, — cries from under the earth, tries to invade their minds.

But they ever ' lay the flattering unction to their souls '. The Prince says :

'. . . there is nothing either good or bad, but thinking makes it so ' (II, 2).

And earlier in the same scene, Polonius comforts himself for his straying wits by saying ' How pregnant sometimes his Replies are ! A happinesse that often Madnesse hits on, which Reason and Sanity could not so prosperously be deliver'd of.'

In *King Lear* is ' the darkness of Revelation', as Swinburne said. In *Hamlet* is the light of Revelation — but not the light seen by the Saints.

Over the world of *Hamlet*, unlike the worlds of *Macbeth* and *King Lear*, reigns a perpetual and terrible light — the light of truth, dissolving all into its element.

In this world of terrible light in which even the dead cannot rest in the peace of the grave, Time does not exist : the beat of the verse sometimes loses its pulse, dissolves in the light, changes to the shadowless, timeless clime of prose.

But Hamlet himself is wasted, not only by the ghost returned from the tomb, but by a shadow — the little Spring-ghost, the fertility daemon, the vegetation spirit that was Ophelia, who, like the fertility daemons of all time, would be dressed in flowers and cast into a stream, —

Ophelia, a shade that at first gave him refreshment and oblivion from the all-seeing light. For a little, but not for long. Then she betrays him to the workaday world, — she shuts out him and his terrible dreams :

OPHELIA

He rais'd a sigh so piteous and profound
That it did seeme to shatter all his bulke,
And end his being. That done, he lets me goe,
And with his head over his shoulder turn'd,
He seem'd to find his way without his eyes ;
For out o' doores he went without their helpe,
And to the last bended their light on me (II, 1).

(We may note, here, how pulseless is the verse. A shadow is speaking. When the Ghost speaks — (he who had lived a full and rich life, dying at the height of that richness) there is a pulse about his speech that Death could not destroy. He speaks with a dark voice that has gathered resonance from the metals that shared the darkness in which he has lain. . . . But Ophelia is disembodied as a shade, — for all those impulses of Spring which found their way at last into the scattered words of her madness.)

In the speech quoted above, Ophelia spoke more truly than she knew. (We find often, in Shakespeare, that a phrase holds all the future, a new universe, while the speaker thinks it is but an idle dropping of words, as apparently meaningless as the few heavy drops of rain that come before the thunder, or the little wind that is heard before an earthquake.)

Hamlet did, indeed, find his way without his eyes — hoping to be guided by an inner sense that took the place of sight. Those bodily eyes had looked on Ophelia and on her alone. And now, in the scene of which she spoke, he saw her for the last time. That sigh ended Hamlet's being, — or in any case, that of the Hamlet she had known. He did, in truth, let her go, — back to the world of dust amid which that little shadow had arisen.

G

Once, he had pretended to belong to that world. In a letter which the little childish traitor had given her father, and which was given by him to the Queen, Hamlet had written :

Thine evermore, most deere Lady, whilst this Machine is to him
   (II, 2).

This tells us what Hamlet would have us think — that his heart is merely something to be dissected and its workings observed. Ophelia might have it (for what it is worth). But it is not even a part of him.

And now, even the machine is not for her. When Hamlet says to Ophelia : ' Look you, how cheerfully my Mother lookes, and my Father dyed within's two houres ', she replies, ' Nay, 'tis twice two Moneths, my Lord '. ' So long ? ' asks Hamlet, seeing her for what she is (III, 2).

The soul of every man is a lonely planet, shut off, excepting for the outward view, from every other.

And Hamlet is by now entirely alone, excepting for the Ghost, and his dream-world.

When Rosencrantz and Guildenstern say, ' We'll wait upon you ', Hamlet, the man who could not tell the Dream from the Reality (and that was part of his tragedy), replies, ' No such matter ; I will not sort you with the rest of my servants ; for to speake to you like an honest man, I am most dreadfully attended ' (II, 2).

Here is a double meaning, already noted by commentators : i.e. the obvious physical meaning, and the meaning that the ' bad dreames ' (' I could be bounded in a nutshell, and count myselfe a King of infinite space, were it not that I have bad dreames ', II, 2) are his servants, his dreadful attendants.

But there is a second meaning. ' Truepenny ' was a contemporary word for a faithful servant. . . . Hamlet addressed the ghost as ' Truepenny '. . . .

When Guildenstern, during this conversation, says

' which dreames, indeed, are Ambition, for the very substance of the Ambitious is meerely the shadow of a
Dreame ' — in the first part of the sentence he said more
than he knew. Hamlet's ' bad dreames ', his dreadful
attendants, were indeed Ambition — the ambition to perform an action, dallied with, dwelt on, in the place of
Reality.

But when Hamlet, in reply to Guildenstern, says

A dreame itselfe is but a shadow.

he is giving the dream more reality than Guildenstern knew.
A shadow must be cast by something — it cannot exist
otherwise.

Of Hamlet's strange phrase :

Then are our Beggers bodies, and our Monarchs and outstretch'd Heroes the Beggers' Shadowes (II, 2).

Coleridge said, ' I do not understand it. And Shakespeare
seems to have intended the meaning not to be more than
snatched at :

"By my fey, I cannot reason." '

But are there not very deep meanings ? *i.e.* that the beggars,
alone among all the things of this world, have, through
their sufferings, their destitution, become real ? (Let us
remember certain passages in *King Lear*.) And that the
outstretched hero is but an *idea*, a dream, sprung from out
of the being of suffering humanity, — a shadow, of a giant
size, in appearance greater than the being that cast it, — a
thing that cannot be seized, but that changes with the
changing of the light. Kings and outstretch'd Heroes are
cast by — brought into being by — beggars' necessities.

These shades are cast, in the all-seeing light, upon a
world of dust. For to this, the world has now been changed
— the dust which can be kneaded into crumbling shapes by
Fate or, so Hamlet tells himself, by his own will. By dust

is he persecuted. The speeches of Polonius drift round and round, generally slowly, upon his point, always returning again to the place whence they started, like a swirl of dry dust in a little air.

'Old men and Comets have been rever'd for the same Reason: their long Beards, and Pretences to foretel Events.'[1]

Yet Polonius has a dry and worldly wisdom — one which is the antithesis of the dream-world of Hamlet (erected in a world of dust).

All things are equal — the dream and the reality. But yet, amid the very dust of Death, some form of life survives, however poor; even with dead clay there is no waste:

A man may fishe with the Worme that hath eat of a King, and eat of the fishe that hath fed of that Worme.
KING: What dost thou meane by this?
HAMLET: Nothing but to show you how a King may goe a Progresse through the guts of a Begger (IV, 3).

. . . .

Alexander dyed, *Alexander* was buried, *Alexander* return-eth into dust; the dust is earth; of earth we make Lome, and why of that Lome, whereto he was converted, might they not stop a Beere barrell?
Imperious Caeser, dead and turn'd to clay,
Might stop a hole to keepe the wind away:
O! that that earth which kept the world in awe,
Should patch a Wall to expell the Winter's flaw (V, 1).

Dust, dust, and Man turning to dust. And yet, in that dust, there is the seed of some use. This is ever in Hamlet's mind. And when, in the scene with the grave-diggers, he says 'That Scull had a tongue in it, and could sing once; how the knave jowles it to the ground, as if it were Caine's jaw-bone, that did the first murther', — he is seeing, perhaps, his uncle as he might be. He is seeing, too, man-inflicted

---

[1] Jonathan Swift, *Thoughts on Various Subjects.*

Death overcome by the Death of Nature. He longs for sleep, yet fears it.

I suppose the epitome of the play lies in the words of Hamlet to Horatio :

> Sir, in my heart there was a kind of fighting
> That would not let me sleepe (V, 2);

.   .   .   .   .   .

Hamlet sees in Ophelia the seeds of his mother's sin. Ophelia, grown mad, mingles, in one song, her agony because her love has gone — deserting her for a pilgrimage to a shrine that is strange to her, where they can never meet, — and her grief for her dead father.

She would not know Hamlet again (so changed is he to her) excepting by the marks of a pilgrimage :

> How should I your true love know from another one ?
> By his Cockle hat and staffe and his Sandal shoone (IV, 5).

When, in this song, she came to

> White his Shroud as the Mountaine Snow
> Larded with sweet flowers,
> Which bewept to the grave did not go
> With true-love showres,

I suppose she had been about to say :

> Which bewept to the grave did go
> With true-love showres.

(And to this, Alexander Pope changed the original.) But in the midst of her song, she remembers it is not her love, but an old man, unwept by any but herself, who is dead, and she changes the purport of her song.

Of these snatches of song, some are echoes of old refrains — ' For Bonny Sweet Robin is all my joy ', for instance, — some, outbursts of grief, whirling round and round in her distraught head . . . sometimes swift as the spring rain, and as quickly gone, — sometimes like the wind.

But in the unbearably poignant

> And will he not come againe?

(where, once more, she identifies Hamlet with her father) —

> And will he not come againe?
> And will he not come againe?
>   No, no, he is dead,
>   Go to thy Death-bed,
> He never will come againe.
>
> His Beard was as white as Snow,
> All Flaxen was his Poll;
>   He is gone, he is gone,
>   And we cast away mone;
> God ha' mercy on his Soule —

there is a complete breakdown of the heart. The springs
are broken, the slow grief has pierced through all, destroy-
ing even the impetus that madness had given.

In the midst of her songs, from the pure and unconscious
heart of Spring, from the lips of Ophelia, sounded the
Fertility Song. A light is thrown on the general trend of
this passage, and on the sentences: ' Well, God'ild you.
They say the Owle was a Baker's Daughter. Lord, we
know what we are, but know not what we may be. God
be at your Table ' — by the fact that in the time of Mary I,
a person was arrested for having written that King Philip
preferred bakers' daughters to Queen Mary.

From this we may gather that a baker's daughter was a
synonym, in that age, for a woman of loose character.

If this be so, the phrase has more than one meaning.
The daughter of joy, the light liver, such as Polonius had
feared his daughter might become, has become the har-
binger of death and of woe.

The little Fertility ghost, or Vegetation daemon, the
ghost of Spring, casts herself into the stream, wreathed with
flowers. . . . The fate of all her kind, since the beginning
of Time, was this: to be cast into the sea, or streams, and

to be mourned over. But in this case it is she who brings about her fate.

This play, sprung from the beginnings of Tragedy, from the Ritual plays of Spring (the plays of which the Fertility ghost cast into the stream, and Winter the slayer, form part), ends with a duel between Hamlet and the brother of Ophelia.

Dr. Lewis Richard Farnell, in *Cults of the Greek States* (Vol. V), speaks of a duel between 'the Black Man and the Fair Man', 'or, as Dionysus the nether god of the black goatskin aids Melanthos (the Black Man) we can call it rather a fight between "black god" and fair god. . . .' This was a form of the ritual-fight between winter and spring.

. . . .

Did this play spring from an ancestral memory, coming to the greatest of all human creators through the saps and juices of the earth, the underground voices heard in the Spring? Perhaps. But to this memory is added the wisdom of all the thousands of springs that have budded since the first Spring, and all the complex character and strangeness of the heart of Man.

Note I

To Hamlet his body is dust, — earth — and the ghost of his father is a mole working, secretly, in the darkness of that earth, bringing into being ancestral impulses, dark urgings from forgotten sources in the blood.

Nothing can rest in darkness.

> Well said, old Mole! Canst work i' th' earth so fast?
> A worthy pioneer! (I, 5)

May there not be depths of meaning beneath that phrase? Is not the 'earth' of which Hamlet speaks, his own too-sullied flesh, his body, the nature which governs his body,

in which many things that were hidden are now thrown up
by that old mole, into the light ?

As against this, in the 2nd Folio, we find ' ground '
instead of earth. Still, I think this meaning is implicit,
although in the passage

> Ah, ha, boy! sayest thou so ?   Art thou there, Truepenny ?
> Come on, you heare this fellow in the sellerage ?
> Consent to sweare.

he refers to the actual earth alone.

·   ·   ·   ·   ·   ·

Note II

Commentators have spoken much of the ' Sun-Son '
pun, — ' Too much i' the sun '. This is to be found elsewhere in Shakespeare, in *King Henry the Fifth*, for instance,
— ' the Sun of heaven '; and in Bardolph's description of
Bardolph's nose, ' the Sunne of utter Darknesse ' appears
in the 2nd Folio.

When the pun is used by Hamlet, it has, sometimes, a
terrible significance, as in the appalling words of Hamlet
to Polonius about his daughter — fearful as the diatribe of
Lear against Woman.

> For if the Sun breed Maggots in a dead dog, being a god
> kissing Carrion, — Have you a daughter ?
> POLONIUS :   I have, my lord.
> HAMLET :   Let her not walk i' the Sunne. Conception is a
> blessing; but not as your daughter may conceive. Friend,
> looke to it (II, 2).

' A god kissing Carrion.' Surely ' god ' is correct. It
was so understood by Warburton, in spite of ' good ' being
an original spelling, perhaps arising from a misunder-
standing.

Puns are constant in Shakespeare, and are never the
result of distortion. Nor do they cause distortion.

Coleridge said, ' I could point out puns in Shakespeare where they appear almost as if the first openings of the mouth of Nature '.

.   .   .   .   .   .

Note III. *The Scenes of Ophelia's Madness*

There's rosemary, that's for remembrance.

' Rosemary was anciently supposed to strengthen the memory, and was not only carried at funerals, but worn at weddings. . . .'—MALONE.

There's fennel for you, and columbines.

Greene, in his *Quip for an Upstart Courtier*, 1592, calls fennel, *women's weeds* : ' fit generally for that sex, sith while they are maidens, they wish wantonly '.

Among Turberville's *Epitaphs*, etc., p. 42 b, I likewise find the following mention of fennel :

> Your fennell did declare
> (As simple men can shewe)
> That flattrie in my breast I bear,
> Where friendship ought to grow.
> —STEEVENS

See Florio's *Italian Dictionary*, 1598. ' Dare finocchio, to give fennel — to flatter, to dissemble.'—MALONE.

' The columbine was emblematical of forsaken lovers :

> The columbine in tawny often taken
> Is then ascribed to such as are forsaken.'
> —HOLT WHITE

(Browne's *Britannia's Pastorals*, bk. I, Song II, 1613)

'. . . there's rue for you ; and, here's some for me ? — we may call it, herb of grace o' Sundays.'

The following passage from Greene's *Quip for an Upstart Courtier* will furnish the best reason for calling *rue* ' herb of grace o' Sundays ' : ' Some of them smil'd and said *Rue* was called Herbegrace, which though they scorned in their youth, they might wear in their age, and that it was never too late to say *miserere* '.—HENLEY.

There's a daisie.

Greene, in his *Quip for an Upstart Courtier*, has explained the significance of this flower : ' Next them grew the *dissembling daisie*, to warne such light-o'-love wenches not to trust every faire promise that such amorous bachelors make them '.—HENLEY.

. . . . . .

Note IV

In the 1st Quarto, the scenes are mixed up. Ophelia gives the flowers before her song about St. Valentine's Day. There is no mention of violets.

When Ophelia, in her madness, says ' I would give you some Violets, but they wither'd when my father dyed ' — may not some echo of Laertes' words to her, at parting, have been in her mind ? He had said to her :

> For Hamlet, and the trifling of his favour,
> Hold it a fashion and a toy in Bloud,
> A Violet in the youth of Primy Nature,
> Forward, not permanent ; sweet, not lasting,
> The perfume and suppliance of a minute ;
> No more (I, 3).

Nevermore for her, that fleeting spring, that ' youth of Primy Nature'. Her father was slain by Hamlet, and she must never see him more.

NOTES ON 'OTHELLO' AND 'HAMLET'

'THERE is practically no doubt that *Othello* was the tragedy written next after *Hamlet*. Such external evidence as we possess points to this conclusion, and it is confirmed by similarities of style, diction, and versification, and also by the fact that ideas and phrases of the earlier play are echoed in the later.'—A. C. BRADLEY, *Shakespearean Tragedy*.

Dr. Bradley adds the note :

' One instance is worth pointing out, because the passage in *Othello* has, oddly enough, given trouble. Desdemona says of her maid Barbara, " She was in love, and he she loved proved mad. And did forsake her ! " Theobald changed " mad " to " bad ", Warburton read " And he she loved forsook her and she proved mad ". Johnson said " mad " meant only " wild, frantic, uncertain ". But what Desdemona says of Barbara is just what Ophelia must have said of herself.'

Should this scene have been intended, originally, to form part of *Hamlet*, then I ask myself whether the refrain of ' All a greene Willough must be my Garland ' (although I know the song from which this was taken is of a time before Shakespeare's) may not be one of those strange fore-shadowings of Fate which occur so often in Shakespeare ?

E. S.

VIII

'OTHELLO, THE MOOR OF VENICE'

'THE heart', wrote William Harvey, in a dedication to King Charles the First, ' is the beginning of life, the sun of the microcosm, even as the sun in his turn might well be designated the heart of the world.'

The tragedy of Othello is that of the overthrow of a heart that was a sun, a sun that was a world — ' a fountain of light, rich in fruitful heat . . . called King of Planets for his motion, heart of the world for his power, its eye for his beauty'.[1] Though this ruled over a night-black body.

When Othello said (to Cassio and others) :

The goodnesse of the night upon you, friends !

it might have been his own goodness that he was bestowing upon them.

But this noble nature must be brought to ruin for no reason but that his grandeur offended the baseness of a cloud born from foul vapours.

The greatness and simplicity of Othello are those of Nature before it was altered by civilisation, and his utterances have in them, sometimes the noble heat of the sun under which he was born, sometimes a grave and planetary splendour, sometimes a sonorous and oceanic strength of harmony. They have, as Swinburne said the verse of Homer has, ' the innumerable music of luminous motion, the simplicity and equality of passion and of power ; the majestic monochord heart of [the] verse has the multitudinous measures of the epic sea '.

This is equally true of the *Othello*-verse.

---

[1] Kepler, of the sun, in one of his earlier lectures, quoted by Sir Arthur Eddington, *The Expanding Universe*.

Othello says of the handkerchief which was one of the engines of his ruin :

> 'Tis true ; there's Magicke in the web of it.
> A Sibyll, that had numbred in the world
> The sun to course two hundred compasses,
> In her prophetic furie sow'd the worke ;
> The Wormes were hallowed that did breed the Silke,
> And it was dyede with Mummey which the skilful
> Conserv'd of Maidens' hearts (III, 4).

The whole of this play is dipped in the dyes of the heart. And the rich light from Othello's being seems to colour the saying of his satellites ; as when the Second Gentleman exclaims :

> The wind-shak'd Surge, with high and monstrous Maine,
> Seems to cast water on the burning Beare
> And quench the Guards of the ever-fixed Pole (II, 1) :

In this world of physical splendour, at the moment of the overthrow of his heaven, Othello says :

> Had she been true,
> If heaven would make me such another world
> Of one entyre and perfect Chrysolite,
> I'd not have sold her for it (V, 2).

Nor would he have been surprised at the existence of such a world.

His love is great as the cause of gravity ' that penetrates to the very centre of the Sun and Planets, without suffering the least diminution of its force. . . . So may the gravitation of the earth be caused by the combined condensation of some other like ethereal spirit.' [1]

The love of Othello was such a spirit, 'conserving the shining of the sun ' his heart.

Here is no low jealousy. When Emilia asks :

> Is he not jealous ?

[1] Sir Isaac Newton.

Desdemona replies :

> Who ? he ? I think the Sun where he was born
> Drew all such humors from him.

But he believes that his heaven is turned to earth — all the planetary music then is discordant.

> But there, where I have garner'd up my heart,
> Where either I must live, or bear no life,
> The Fountaine from the which my current runnes
> Or else dries up ; to be discarded thence !
> Or keep it as a Cisterne for foule Toads
> To knot and gender in ! Turne thy complexion there,
> Patience, thou young and rose-lipp'd Cherubim ;
> Ay, there, look grim as hell !

DESDEMONA

I hope my noble lord esteems me honest.

OTHELLO

> O ! ay ; as Sommer flies are in the Shambles,
> That quicken even with blowing. O thou Weed !
> Who art so lovely faire and smellst so sweete
> That the Sence aches at thee, would thou hadst ne'er
>   been born ! (IV, 2)

His love, young and golden-haired as Proserpine, has changed to

>   . . . that cunning whore of Venice
> That married with Othello. You, Mistris,
> That have the office opposite to Saint Peter,
> And keepe the Gate of Hell.

From the moment of doubting, Othello speaks of himself, often, as if the Othello he had once known, the Othello whom the world had known, were a person divided from him ; or he speaks as a dead man might speak, watching the intolerable anguish of the living — he does not say ' I ', he says ' Othello '.[1]

Othello's Occupation's gone ! (III, 3)

[1] This habit appears elsewhere in Shakespeare. But in the case of Othello, it has a particularly agonising effect.

He utters this terrible cry :

> Where should Othello goe ? (V, 2)

But, a little later, in

> That's he that was Othello ; heere I am,

he seems to have taken farewell of himself for ever. Only
in the extremity of anguish will that dead man become the
living man again. Even in the quieter, less terrible

> Then, must you speake
> Of one that loved not wisely but too well ;
> Of one not easily jealous, but being wrought,
> Perplex'd in the extreme ; of one whose hand,
> Like the base Indian, threw a Pearle away
> Richer than all his Tribe ; of one whose subdu'd Eyes,
> Albeit unused to the melting moode,
> Drop teares as fast as the Arabian Trees
> Their med'cinable gumme (V, 2).

> .   .   .   .

When not goaded by that gadfly Iago into some hurried
utterance, even in the depths of his misery, his speeches
have that grave and planetary measure, that unhurried
splendour of utterance, which seems a part of his nature.

> It is the Cause, it is the Cause, my soule ; —
> Let me not name it to you, you chaste Starres !
> It is the Cause.   Yet I'll not shed her blood,
> Nor scarre that whiter skin of hers than Snow,
> And smooth as monumental Alabaster.
> Yet she must dye, else she'll betray more men.
> Put out the Light, and then put out the Light :
> If I quench thee, thou flaming Minister,
> I can againe thy former light restore,
> Should I repent me : but once put out thy Light,
> Thou cunningst Patterne of excelling Nature,
> I know not where is that Promethean heate
> That can thy Light relume.   When I have pluck'd the Rose
> I cannot give it vitall growth againe,
> It needs must wither : I'll smell it on the tree.

> O balmy breath, that dost almost persuade
> Justice to breake her Sword ! One more, one more.
> Be thus when thou art dead, and I will kill thee,
> And love thee after. One more, and this the last :
> So sweet was ne'er so fatall. I must weepe,
> But they are cruell Teares ; this sorrow's heavenly ;
> It strikes where it doth love (V, 2).

Othello had said, kissing his love,

> And this, and this, the greatest discords be
> That e'er our hearts shall make ! (II, 1)

It is this harmony that must be broken by Iago :

> O ! You are well tun'd now,
> But Ile set downe the pegges that make this Musicke,
> As honest as I am.

In the more noble passages of Othello's anger, the torture appears, in the very sound of the verse :

> If I do prove her Haggard,
> Though that her Jesses were my deere heart-strings,
> I'd whistle her off and let her downe the winde,
> To prey at Fortune. Haply, for I am blacke,
> And have not those soft parts of Conversation
> That Chamberers have, or, for I am declin'd
> Into the vale of years — yet that's not much —
> She's gone ; I am abus'd ; and my releefe
> Must be to loathe her. O Curse of Marriage !
> That we can call these delicate Creatures ours,
> And not their Appetites ! I had rather be a Toad,
> And live upon the Vapour of a Dungeon,
> Than keepe a corner in the thing I love
> For others' uses. Yet 'tis the plague of Great Ones ;
> Prerogativ'd are they lesse than the Base ;
> 'Tis destiny unshunnable, like death :
> Even then this forked plague is Fated to us
> When we do quicken.
>   Look ! Where she comes.
> If she be false, O ! then heaven mocked itself.
> Ile not believe it ! (III, 3)

(' Mocked ', I think, and not ' mocks ' as appears in modern editions. The meaning, surely, is that Heaven mocked itself in the making of Desdemona.)

' This forked plague ' seems at once the horns of the deceived . . . the forked tongue of the serpent who brought about the Fall of Man . . . the serpent tongue of Iago. . . .

We have seen, already, that in the earlier lines :

> Excellent wretch ! Perdition catch my Soule,
> But I do love thee ! And when I love thee not,
> Chaos is come againe ! (III, 3)

the pause between ' wretch ' and ' Perdition ' is like a whirl-pool or vortex. In the first line of the passage quoted above, the word ' Haggard ' swirls round on itself; the feeling has found words, found reality — that feeling which was unspoken and terrible in the swirling movement of the caesura to which I have just referred. The word ' Appe-tites ' is like something broken into bits, and tossed, at the end, into the empty air.

With the a-sounds echoing each other, of ' plague of Great Ones ', ' Even then this forked plague is Fated to us ' — fires seem breaking from the nature of Othello, those fires of the African which had long been covered by civilisation, — or ' the Sun's advance towards the Earth, or such a rupture of the Earth as will let out the Central Fires '.

This was now the fate of Othello. His complete dis-integration is echoed and mirrored in the very sound of the verse.

High a-sounds occurred previously in the speech, in ' prey ' (where the e takes on the sound of a), in ' Conversa-tion ' and ' Chamberers '. But later, these had a different effect, were, perhaps, even more terrible. The muttering sounds of ' Conversation ', ' Chamberers ', are like dust gathering itself into shape. For Othello is slowly being

H

changed by the forked plague, into the likeness of that
being of the 24th canto of the *Inferno* :

> ' Nè *o* sì tosto mai nè *i* si scrisse,
> Com' el s' accese ed arse, e cener tutto
> Convenne che cascando divenisse ;
> E poi che fu a terra sì distrutto,
> La polver si raccolse per sè stessa,
> E 'n quel medesmo ritornò di butto.' [1]

As Othello speaks the words ' the plague of Great Ones '
his torture touches all extremes.

OTHELLO

O blood, blood, blood.

IAGO

Patience, I say, your minde, perhaps, may change.

OTHELLO

Never, Iago. Like to the Ponticke Sea,
Whose icie current and compulsive course
Ne'er feeles returning ebbe, but keepes due on
To the Proponticke and the Hellespont,
Even so, my bloody thoughts, with violent pace,
Shall ne'er looke backe, ne'er ebbe to humble love,
Till that a capable and wide Revenge
Swallow them up.
                    Now, by yond Marble Heaven,
In the due reverence of a Sacred vow
I heere engage my words (III, 3),

— the pause following ' Never, Iago ' is like a solar cyclone,
and its centre, as with that phenomenon, seems of an
appalling coldness and darkness. (The central region of a
solar cyclone [2] — ' must be a region of refrigeration '.

---

[1]
> ' Never " O " nor " I " was written in such a gust
> Of speed as he took fire with, all allumed,
> And then must needs drop into ash and dust,
> When down to the very ground he was consumed,
> Of its own motion re-combining there,
> The dust straightway its former shape resumed.'
> —Trans. L. Binyon.

[2] Herbert Spencer.

' Just where there would exist a . . . prolongation of the
cyclonic cloud down towards the sun's body, the darkness
is greater than elsewhere. . . .

'. . . In a whirlwind, as in a whirlpool, the vortex will
be below the general level, and all around the surface of the
medium will descend towards it.')

We have met a pause like a cyclone before, in Shakespeare. But that was not cold, nor did it suck all down
into its depth. Once, when the fires from his own nature,
the mineral poison of Iago, have reduced him to dust, — the
dust that was Othello, as it re-forms, takes on almost
the likeness of Iago, speaks almost with his voice, — as
in the speech : ' Handkerchief, — Confessions — Handkerchief ! To confess, and be hanged for his labour. First,
to be hanged, and then to confess : I tremble at it. . . .'
Here, and throughout this passage, his very speech is
shrunken, corroded, shrivelled by that poison, — is dwindled
down into shapeless prose. But elsewhere, almost always,
in this agony, there are the glorious dyes of the heart, the
light from that world which might have been ' of an intire
and perfect Chrysolite '.

Only at the end, when all the blood from Othello's heart
has flown, knowing the being he loved and has slain was
innocent, are all the bright dyes gone.

> . . . O ill-starr'd wench !
> Pale as thy Smocke ! When we shall meet at Compt,
> This looke of thine will hurle my soule from Heaven,
> And fiends will snatch at it. Cold, cold, my Girle !
> Even like thy Chastity.

But even then, before his death, the richness and the
grandeur return to

> . . . one whose subdu'd Eyes,
> Albeit unused to the melting moode,
> Drop teares as fast as the Arabian Trees
> Their med'cinable gumme.

Iago has killed this world for him, but not the next. In the lines :

> When we shall meet at Compt,
> This looke of thine will hurle my soule from Heaven,
> And fiends will snatch at it.

he is still Iago's property : he blackens Desdemona's heavenly love. But in the last lines :

> I kist thee ere I kill'd thee ; no way but this,
> Killing myselfe, to dye upon a kisse.

he has gone to join her, in a world of which Iago's mind could have no conception.

. . . .

Ludovici, apostrophising Iago, cried ' O Spartan dog ! '

More fell than Anguish, Hunger, or the Sea :

and almost all commentators have written of Iago's ' greatness ' — Swinburne saying that ' Desdemona was between the devil and the deep sea '. There he is right, and Mr. Wilson Knight speaks with equal truth when he calls Iago ' the spirit of negation '.[1]

Iago appears in a shrunken shape, with a dulled and hooded eye, as the first tempter appeared in Eden. With the exception of two earth-shaking sentences, and one speech of great beauty in which his voice has taken on the sound of Othello's, Iago never speaks ' above a mortal mouth '. For the rest, there is in his verbal intercourse with others, the terrible ' deadness ' that Dr. Bradley noted in the *feeling* of Iago.

He is a subterranean devil. . . . His voice comes to us muffled by the earth of the world and of his nature. It comes to us from underground, like that of the ' old mole ' that Hamlet knew. That is why it sounds so small. But it is none the less deadly. Iago is a million miles beneath the surface of our nature. Though ineffably tainted by the

[1] *The Wheel of Fire.*

world's evil, he is so shut off from the world of ordinary men — he who is yet shaping their lives — that he cannot reach them by any words save those with a jet of poison in them. Though he can overthrow them with a touch, it hardly seems to be *his* touch.

He cannot express himself. ‘Do not weep, do not weep ! Alas the day ! ’ (IV, 2) he says to Desdemona after the scene when she first realises that night is falling.

Indeed, he does not need her tears. They give him no particular pleasure : if anything, they disturb him in his intellectual pride at what he has done.

In one gigantic phrase (as Bradley and other commentators have pointed out) Iago acknowledges the race from which he has sprung — his birth-place, and home. In answer to Othello's

> I looke downe towards his feet ; but that's a fable.
> If that thou beest a divell, I cannot kill thee.

comes Iago's

> I bleed, sir ; but not kill'd.

Bradley writes : ‘He is saying, you see, he is right, I am a devil ’.

But it goes even further than that. He seems surprised, almost, at that one signal proof that he is man as well as devil : his blood.

This gigantic avowal is equalled by the earlier

> I am your owne for ever (III, 3) —

echoing the still more appalling words of Othello's

> I am bound to thee for ever (III, 3).

Othello saw in those words no particular significance. Now, as Iago echoed that avowal, Othello, going through the door, did not hear the words telling him that through the rest of eternity they will be companions in Hell, as tormented and tormentor — that Othello has come down to Iago, and that Iago is attached to him as the serpent is to the heel of the first man.

Before these world-shaking acknowledgments of Iago's devilship, there has been a subterranean hint of the race from which he sprang :

OTHELLO

O misery !

IAGO

Poore and Content is rich, and rich enough,
But riches finelesse is as poore as Winter
To him that ever feares he shall be poore.
Good heaven, the Soules of all my Tribe defend
From jealousie ! (III, 3)

Here, perhaps, he is saying that the devils are not so forsaken by Heaven that Heaven will not defend them from the worst of all miseries.

Once, and once only, Iago speaks with the voice of a free man :

Not Poppy, nor Mandragora,
Nor all the drowsy Syrups of the world,
Shall ever medicine thee to that sweete sleepe
Which thou ow'dst yesterday (III, 3).

This, in its profound beauty, its heart-shaking simplicity, is almost like a foreshadowing of Othello's

O ! now, for ever
Farewell the Tranquill minde ; farewell Content !
Farewell the plumed Troope and the bigge Warres
That make Ambition Virtue ! O, farewell !
Farewell the neighing Steed, and the shrill Trumpe,
The spirit-stirring Drum, the eare-piercing Fife,
The Royall banner, and all Quality,
Pride, Pomp, and Circumstance of glorious Warre !
And, O you mortall Engines, whose rude throates
The immortal Jove's dread clamours counterfeit,
Farewell ! Othello's Occupation's gone ! (III, 3)

In the speech of Iago there was no exultance, — only the freedom of one whose task is done. A human voice is speaking : for once Iago has understood suffering, and the blood which has given him the semblance of a living being voices itself.

In nearly all other passages, even in

> Witnesse, you ever-burning Lights above !
> You Elements that clip us round about !
> Witnesse, that heere Iago doth give up
> The execution of his wit, hands, heart,
> To wrong'd Othello's service (III, 3),

— his speech is shrunken and bloodless, like the slough cast by a snake.

Once he is frightened — when Othello warns him :

> If thou dost slander her and torture me,
> Never pray more ; Abandon all remorse ;
> On Horror's head Horrors accumulate ;
> Doe deeds to make Heaven weepe, all Earth amaz'd ;
> For nothing canst thou to damnation adde
> Greater than that (III, 3).

Then, Iago's speech becomes a dirty, small, and fluttering thing, like a poisonous insect :

> O grace ! O heaven forgive me !
> Are you a man ? Have you a Soule or Sense ?
> God be wi' you ; take mine office. O wretched Foole !
> That liv'st to make thine Honesty a Vice.
> O monstrous world ! Take note, take note, O world !
> To be direct and honest is not safe.
> I thanke you for this profit, and, from hence
> Ile love no friend, sith love breeds such offence (III, 3).

It is through the very deadness of his speech that his creator expresses him.

He scarcely cares who he injures, so long as an injury is done, and by his hand. In the first scene of the play, he says

> Call up her father ;
> Rouse him, make after him, poyson his delight,
> Proclaime him in the streets, Incense her kinsmen,

And, though he in a fertile clymate dwell,
Plague him with Flyes ; though that his joy be joy,
Yet throw such changes of vexation on't
As it may lose some colour.

' *Plague him with Flyes.*' Indeed, he lives in a world of flies.

What is this hell, this world of flies, which he inhabits as the devil of his own pain ?   Is it pride — as almost every critic has held ?   Is pride his element, his climate, and his eternity ?

' If, of that which this heart of mine is feeling, one drop were to fall into hell, hell itself would become all life eternal. . . .'   Thus spoke St. Catherine of Genoa. . . . The ' life eternal ' is union with God. . . . One drop from the darkness of Iago would raise all hell to the rebellion against God.

For Iago does not feel (as Bradley has pointed out). . . . I would add the suggestion that this may be one reason why he wishes to injure mankind, which possesses the power to feel, to suffer — that power which he lacks.

For he must be first in everything, — and to lack anything, even the power of feeling, is to be inferior.

Roderigo says to him, of Othello,

Thou toldst me thou didst hold him in thy hate.

And Iago replies,

Despise me if I doe not (I, 1).

To be despised, is Death.

Iago is, perhaps, too far under the earth for hatred. . . . But pride, he tells himself, must surely give him *some* feeling : he owes it to his pride to hate.

And he is filled with an immeasurable contempt : but this is scarcely a *feeling.*

To Roderigo he says (I, 3),

What sayst thou, noble heart ?

And by the very fact of applying the words to that despised

being, he tells us what is his opinion of a noble heart.

He has a curiosity to see what will be the movements, under pain, of these extraordinary beings of an alien world — beings who have passions, nobilities, and are ruled by a power that is not that of the will.

Sometimes he even tries to emulate their feelings, the speech born from these, — as when he pretends to himself, and to Emilia, that he knows jealousy — (but even then the pretence breaks down, and we see the face behind the mask : it is that of Pride) — or as when, in the first scene, he says :

> Though I doe hate him as I doe hell-pains.

But here, we feel that he is disguising from us that those pains are his climate — he is used to them, is a native of them ; they do not touch him as they would those who have hearts to be consumed. He would, indeed, hardly know the difference between those pains and the pleasures of heaven. For he is not a damned soul. He is a devil.

He lives by the will — that self-will which, the saints tell us, causes our perpetual separation from God.

'Vertue ! a figge ! 'tis in ourselves that we are thus, or thus. Our Bodies are our Gardens, to the which our wills are Gardiners ; So that if wee will plant Nettles or sowe Lettice, set Hyssope and weed up Time, Supply it with one Gender of Hearbes or distract it with many, either to have it sterril with idleness or manured with Industry, why the power and corrigible authority of this lies in our wills. If the balance [1] of our lives had not one scale of Reason to poyse another of Sensuality, the blood and baseness of our Natures would conduct us to most preposterous Conclusions ; but wee have reason to coole our raging Motions, our carnall Stings, our unbitted Lusts, whereof I take this that you call Love, to be a Sect or Seyen ' (I, 3).

He seems, in his curiosity, to be asking for information about this strange stirring in the being.

[1] ' balance '. In the 1632 Folio, it is ' braine '.

Once, he almost believes (coldly and curiously) that he himself feels this stirring :

> . . . That Cassio loves her, I do well beleeve it ;
> That she loves him, 'tis apt, and of great credite ;
> The Moore (howbeit that I endure him not)
> Is of a constant, loving, noble Nature ;
> And I dare thinke he'le prove to Desdemona
> A most deare husband. Now, I doe love her too ;
> Not out of absolute lust — (though peradventure
> I stand accountant for as great a sinne) —
> But partly led to dyet my Revenge,
> For that I doe suspect the lusty Moore
> Hath leap'd into my seat ; the thought whereof
> Doth like a poisonous Minerall gnaw my Inwards ;
> And nothing can or shall content my Soule
> Till I am eeven'd with him, wife for wife ;
> Or failing so, yet that I put the Moore
> At least into a Jealousie so strong
> That Judgment cannot cure (II, 1).

To him, the destruction of Hell is always cold — that of a poisonous mineral — is never that of fire, since fire purifies :

> The Moore already changes with my poyson :
> Dangerous conceites are in their Natures poysons,
> Which at the first are scarce found to distaste,
> But with a little act upon the blood,
> Burne like the Mines of Sulphure (III, 3).

Even at that moment when his pride tells him there is a stirring in his nature, ' not out of absolute lust ' he does not know feeling.

When Othello, in the midst of his torture, falls into a coma, following the words ' Confess — ! Handkerchief — ! O divell ! ' (IV, 1), Iago says : ' How is it, Generall ? Have you not hurt your head ? ' and Othello, from his mine of sulphur, replies ' Dost thou mocke me ? '

Iago is honestly surprised by the question.

> I mocke you ? No, by heaven.

For how should he understand the agony of the soul ?

Yet he knows there is a difference between himself and the common humanity who feel that ' Sect or Seyen ' of lust that they call love ; he realises even, in a numb way, that they do not recognise it as only a freak of nature, a sport of that greater parent :

CASSIO :   She's a most exquisite Lady.
IAGO :   And, Ile warrant her, full of Game.
CASSIO :   Indeed, she is a most fresh and delicate Creature.
IAGO :   What an eye she has ! methinkes it sounds a parley of
 provocation.
CASSIO :   An inviting eye : and yet methinkes right modest.
IAGO :   And when she speakes, is it not an Alarum to love ?
CASSIO :   She is indeed perfection (II, 3).

This difference between their point of view was, perhaps, the

> . . . daily beauty in his life
> That makes me ugly (V, 1),

— and the reason why Cassio must die.

For at one moment, Iago had thought it would not be worth while to kill Cassio. If he lived or died would be indifferent to Iago, who is not a murderer for the sake of murder, but ' an intellectual following his philosophical tenets to their logical conclusion '.

> Though in the trade of warre I have slaine men,
> Yet doe I hold it very stuffe o' the conscience
> To doe no contriv'd murder : I lacke iniquitie
> Sometimes to doe me service (I, 2).

This is his one fault, perhaps, according to his own tenets : his one failure to serve his god, — Himself.

Iago sees himself as good as any man. (For does he not follow the tenets of his religion, evolved from his own nature ?) Or, at any rate, he believes that the ' good heaven ' may ' the souls of all my tribe defend '. Like the fallen angels, he tells himself that he has a right to heaven.

But he is not a fallen being . . . he has never known either the Paradise of the first man, or the heaven of the angels. When Cassio is drunk (II, 3) he says to Iago :

> Well, God's above all; and there be soules must be saved, and there be soules must not be saved.

Iago, amused, answers :

> It's true, good lieutenant.
> CASSIO : For mine owne part — no offence to the Generall nor any man of quality — I hope to be saved.
> IAGO : And so doe I too, lieutenant.
> CASSIO : Ay; but by your leave, not before me; the lieutenant is to be saved before the Ancient.

This speech with its reminder of injuries that Iago thought he had suffered, and the claim that Iago might not be first in heaven (as he was first in hell), acted on Iago like the poison from the mines of sulphur. Remembered at the moment of decision, it determined Iago that Cassio must die. These words came from a being whom Iago despised, but who had been put before him and had reminded him of that preferment.

To Montana, who had been watching Cassio, he said :

> You see this fellow that is gone before ;
> He is a Soldier fit to stand by Caesar
> And give direction : and doe but see his vice ;
> 'Tis to his vertue a just Equinox,
> The one as long as the other ; 'tis pity of him (II, 3).

For he, Iago, has no vice. To have a vice would be to sink below the strength of his will. Pride is the virtue of the devils : and to be a villain in the ordinary sense is beneath the dignity of the Princes of Hell.

Indeed, to bring about his own ends, Iago can even assume a virtue :

> How poore are they that have not Patience !

he says to Roderigo (II, 3). And his own patience is endless.

'His creed,' says Bradley, 'for he is no sceptic, he has a definite creed, is that absolute egoism is the only natural and proper attitude, and that conscience or honour or any other kind of regard for others is an absurdity.'

'O! villainous' (he exclaims, when Roderigo threatens to drown himself because of his unrequited passion for Desdemona). 'I have looked upon the world for four times seven years, and since I could distinguish betwixt a benefit and an injury, I never found a man that knew how to love himselfe. Ere I would say I would drowne myselfe for the love of a Gynney Hen, I would change my humanity with a Baboone' (I, 3).

It is to be noted here, that whilst most men would say 'Since I could distinguish right from wrong', Iago says 'distinguish benefit from injury'.

And yet, for all his self-love, this creature who in spite of his shrunken speech has what Baudelaire called 'la vraie grandeur des pariahs', in order to bring about damnation in the world, is willing to forfeit his own life. He scarcely cares. 'In more than one way', said St. Augustine, 'do men sacrifice to the rebellious angels.'

As commentators have pointed out, Iago is perfectly honest in many of his speeches about himself. 'Men should be what they seem', he says of Cassio. Iago is what he seems : but nobody will believe him. It is impossible that a man should impute such a character to himself, did it exist.

Iago says to Othello : 'My Lord, you know I love you' (III, 3). He does not say : 'I love you. . . .' And there must have been laughter in Hell at those words.

Sometimes, however, as all writers on Shakespeare have discerned, Iago looks from behind a grave mask, swearing 'By Janus', and smiling to think we do not see the two faces of the god who is his patron and pattern — the god of the door, the gateway. . . . We know whither that door led, in Othello's case. . . .

But Iago's speech, as I have said already, is no mask.

'The degree and nature of a man's sensibility', said Nietzsche, in *Beyond Good and Evil*, ' extends to the highest altitude of his spirit.'—Iago's did not. He is slow and sluggish as the serpent. When he speaks in verse, there is scarcely a beat or pulse, excepting when he is speaking of himself. The movement of the verse is horizontal, never vertical.

In spite of this pulselessness, the caesura is at times so deep that we feel we are looking down into a chasm of Hell.

> I am glad of it ; for now I shall have reason
> To show the Love and Duty that I beare you
> With franker spirit ; therefore, as I am bound,
> Receive it from me ; I speake not yet of proofe.
> Looke to your wife ; observe her well with Cassio ;
> Weare your eyes thus, not jealous nor Secure :
> I would not have your free and Noble Nature
> Out of selfe-Bounty be abus'd ; look to't (III, 3).

Down to ' abus'd ' all the caesuras are equal, — moderately long, — the ordinary breaks of speech. But with that word, we look down into a hell-chasm, — but only for a moment. The pause, though of that depth, is scarcely longer than the others.

After this speech, for a while, the pauses are less deep, — and are quick, as if Iago were covering up something, as in

> He thought 'twas witchcraft ; but I am much to blame.

In the following lines :

> I hope you will consider what is spoke
> Comes from my love. But I do see y'are moov'd (III, 3),

— after the huddled movement of the first line, comes, in the second, another deep chasm, — that, perhaps, of the Hell from which Iago was born. That dulled speech of his causes him to repeat ' I see y'are moov'd ' once again within the space of nine lines.

.   .   .   .   .   .

How strangely must Iago and Desdemona have looked into each other's eyes.

'For,' as Jeremy Taylor said of a gaze, ' as from the eyes of some persons, there shoots forth an evil influence, and some have an evil eye and are infectious, some look truthfully as a friendly planet, and innocent as flowers.'

Desdemona, this young being who said of her hand

It yet has felt no age nor knowne no sorrow (III, 4),

— she whose ' sins ' were ' loves she bore ' Othello ; she who was ' a child to chiding ', and who must go into the darkness alone, — saw no treachery in Iago.

' In the seventh story of the third decade of the Hecatom-mithi of M. Giovanbattista Giralda Cinthio, nobile Fer-rarese ', first published in 1565 (said Swinburne, in *Three Plays of Shakespeare*), ' there is an incident so beautifully related that it seems at first inexplicable that Shakespeare, when engaged in transfiguring this story into the tragedy of Othello, can have struck it out of his version. The loss of the magic handkerchief which seals the doom of the hero and his fellow-victim is far less plausibly and far less beautifully explained by a mere accident, and a most un-likely accident, than by a device which heightens at once the charm of Desdemona and the atrocity of Iago. It is through her tenderness for his little child that he takes occasion to destroy her.

' The ancient, or ensign . . . is, of course, if compared with Iago, a mere shadow cast before it by the advent of that awful figure. But none the less is he the remarkably powerful and original creature of a true and tragic genius.

. . . .

' This plain and natural motive would probably have sufficed for any of those great contemporaries who find it easier to excel all other tragic and comic poets since the passing of Sophocles and Aristophanes, than to equal or draw near to Shakespeare. For him it was insufficient.

' Neither envy nor hatred nor jealousy nor resentment, all at work together in festering confusion of anxious and

contemplative evil, can quite explain Iago even to himself.
Yet neither Macbeth nor even Hamlet is by nature more
inevitably introspective. But the secret of the abyss of this
man's nature lies deeper than did ever plummet sound save
Shakespeare's. The bright and restless devil of Goethe's
invention, the mournful and more majestic devil created
by Marlowe, are spirits of less deep damnation than that
incarnate in the bluff, plain-spoken soldier whose honesty
is the one obvious thing about him, the one unmistakable
quality which neither man nor woman ever fails to recognise
and to trust.

' And what is even the loftier Faust, whose one fitting
mate was Helen, if compared with the subjects of Iago's
fathomless and bottomless malice ?

'Shakespeare alone could have afforded to cancel the most
graceful touch, to efface the loveliest feature, in the sketch
of Cinthio's heroine. But Desdemona can dispense with
even this.

' " The Moor's wife went often, as I have said, to the
ancient's wife's house and abode with her a good part of the
day. Whence this man seeing that she sometimes bore
about her a handkerchief which he knew that the Moor had
given her, the which handkerchief was wrought in Moorish
wise most subtly, and was most dear to the lady, and in
like wise to the Moor, he bethought him to take it from her
secretly, and thence to prepare against her her final ruin.
And he having a girl of three years old, which child was
much beloved of Desdemona, one day that the hapless lady
had gone to stay in the house of this villain, he took the
little girl in his arms and gave her to the lady, who took
her and gathered her to her breast : this deceiver who was
excellent at sleight of hand, reft from her girdlestead the
handkerchief so cunningly that she was in no whit aware
of it, and departed from her right joyful. Desdemona,
knowing not this, went home, and being busied with other
thoughts took no heed of the handkerchief. But some days

thence, seeking for it and not finding it, she was right fearful lest the Moor should ask it of her, as he was often wont to do."

'The reader of this terribly beautiful passage cannot fail to ask himself why Shakespeare forbore to make use of it. . . .

'There is but one [reason] ; but it is all-sufficient. In Shakespeare's world, as in nature's, it is impossible that monsters should propagate : that Iago should beget, or that Goneril or Regan should bring forth. Their children are creatures unimaginable to man.'

   .   .   .   .

'An eye', said Jeremy Taylor, 'that dwells too long upon a starre must be refreshed with lesser beauties, and strengthened with greens and looking glasses, lest the sight become amazed with too great a splendour.'

The beauty is no less, but the ineffable drooping swan-like dying music of Desdemona is in contrast to the planetary magnificence of Othello's gait in verse :

> I cannot weepe, nor answer have I none,
> But what should go by water. . . . (IV, 2).

and

> Sing all a greene willough shall be my garland (IV, 3).

— these are in the same tones.

> It is the wind.

— a dropping and dying fall, bringing memories of sweetness. Yes. 'It is the wind.' Only that, and as swiftly gone. Her words were always few, and always had the sound of a wind among trees.

Sometimes the very sound of her voice will bring a faint echo of that of her beloved Othello :

OTHELLO

Ah ! Desdemona ; away, away, away !

DESDEMONA

Alas, the heavy day ! — Why do you weepe ? (IV, 2)

I

An echo, more than a rhyme ; and one deep in her heart,
as the echoing sound lies deep in the line.

NOTE TO ' OTHELLO '

ACT I, SCENE I

And, though he in a fertile Clymate dwell,
Plague him with Flyes. . . .

JEAN WIERUS, pupil of Agrippa, gives the following names
as being among the Powers and Principalities of Hell.

BEELZEBUB : Supreme Chief of the Infernal Court and Empire,
and Founder of the Order of the Fly.

LEONARD : Grand Master of the Sabbath, Knight of the Fly.

CHAMOS : Knight of the Fly.

(Jean Wierus, — 'Des prestiges des démons.' Cinq livres
de l'imposture et tromperie des diables, des enchantements
et sorcelleries. Fait français par Jacques Grévin de
Chermant. Paris, 1569.)

IX

'TIMON OF ATHENS'

SWINBURNE, writing of Chapman's translation of Homer, said, ' His fiery and turbid style has in it the action rather of earthquakes and volcanoes than of the oceanic verse . . .' (of Homer). ' It can show but the huge movements of the heaving earth, inflated and inflamed with unequal and violent life, for the innumerable unity and harmony, the radiant and buoyant music of luminous motion, the simplicity and equality of passion and of power, the majestic monochord of single sound underlying as it were the multitudinous measures of the epic sea.'

This passage might equally be applied to the difference between the splendours of *Othello* and the turgid magnificence of *Timon of Athens*, where the earth-shaking rumblings seem to come from the deepest heart of Nature.

> That Nature, being sicke of man's Unkindnesse,
> Should yet be hungry! Common Mother, thou   (*Digging*)
> Whose Wombe Unmeasurable, and infinite breast,
> Teemes and feedes all ; whose selfe-same Mettle
> Whereof thy proud Child, arrogant man, is puft,
> Engenders the blacke Toad and Adder blew,
> The gilded Newt and eyelesse venom'd Worme,
> With all the abhorred Births below crispe Heaven,
> Whereon Hyperion's quickening fire doth shine ;
> Yeald him, who all thy human Sonnes doth hate,
> From foorth thy plenteous bosome, one poore roote ! (IV, 3)

Here, in the 3rd, 4th, and 8th lines, the sound is turgid and rumbling as if it preceded an earthquake.

This play of

. . . Fools of fortune, trencher-friends, Time's flies (III, 6),

and of one who came to this change

> As the Moore doe's, by wanting light to give :
> But then renew I could not like the Moone ;
> There were no Sunnes to borrow of (IV, 3),

bears a prophetic colouring of the present age, — of

> Flinty mankinde ; whose eyes do never give,
> But thorough Lust and Laughter. Pittie's sleeping :
> Strange times, that weepe with laughing, not with weeping
> (IV, 3).

In this poem ' inspired at once ', as Swinburne said, ' by
the triune Furies of Ezekiel, of Juvenal, and of Dante ',
— in the Fifth Act, as Swinburne thinks (and, I would
suggest, in the Fourth also, beyond any reasonable doubt),
the presence of Shakespeare ' predominates generally over
the sullen and brooding atmosphere, with the fierce imperious glare of a " bloody sun " like that which the wasting
seamen watched at noon " in a hot and copper sky " ' .

But even here the noble man does not descend to the
company of the beasts ; the difference is shown between
the man who hates through his excess of love, shattered in
his breast, and the man whose hatred is a negation of life.

TIMON : What wouldst thou do with the world, Apemantus, if
it lay in thy power ?
APEMANTUS : Give it to the Beasts, to be rid of the men.
TIMON : Wouldst thou have thy selfe fall in the confusion of
men, and remaine a Beast with the Beasts ?
APEMANTUS : I, Timon.
TIMON : A beastly Ambition, which the Goddes grant thee to
attaine to.

. . . .

What Beast couldst thou bee, that were not subject to a
Beast ? And what a Beast art thou already, that seest not
thy losse in transformation ! (IV, 3)

Nothing is wasted, excepting Time's flies, that vanish
like the vapours to which they are compared. The very
fires of Timon's hatred weld weak evil into a strong and
active good :

TIMON (*to the thieves*)

The Sunne's a Theefe, and with his great attraction
Robbes the vast Sea ; the Moone's an arrant Theefe,
And her pale fire she snatches from the Sunne ;
The Sea's a Theefe, whose liquid Surge resolves
The Moon into Salte teares ; the Earth's a Theefe,
That feeds and breeds by a composture stolne
From general excrement. . . . (IV, 3).

But in answer to this, and to Timon's exhortation to continue in their Roguery, the thieves reply thus :

THIRD THIEF :   He has almost charmed me from my Profession
by persuading me to it.

FIRST THIEF :   'Tis in the malice of mankinde that he thus
advises vs ; not to have vs thrive in our mystery.

SECOND THIEF :   I'll beleeve him as an Enemy, and give over
my Trade.

FIRST THIEF :   Let vs first see peace in Athens ; there is no
time so miserable but a man be true.

I do not understand the last sentence. Did the First
Thief mean that he would resign his ' mystery ', in order
to do his duty to the city that bred him ? Or was Shakespeare speaking, through the thief's lips, with a terrible
irony ? Did the thief mean that he would be true to his
own villainy ?

But all comes to an end, and Nature, in her wisdom,
forgives all.

In Alcibiades' words over the tomb of Timon, lies the
epitome of the poem :

Though thou abhorrd'st in vs our humane griefes,
Scornd'st our Braine's flow and those our droplets which
From niggard Nature fall, yet rich Conceit
Taught thee to make vast Neptune weepe for aye
On thy low grave, on faults forgiven. . . . (V, 4).

X

A NOTE ON 'MEASURE FOR MEASURE'

I PLACE this play among the Tragedies, for that, in effect, is what it is.

Measure for Measure is, perhaps, the only generation born of the Cold to be found in the work of Shakespeare.

At first sight it appears cold as the brain of Justice, hard and perfect as a hailstone might be, were this not ephemeral and small, but vast and everlasting as a meteoric boulder.

But this is because the coldness of human justice is contrasted with the great mercy of God.

Excepting in Claudio, the condemned sinner, it is Sin that is cold — all the heat and marrow of youth are gone.

Lucio says :

> Thy bones are hollow : Impiety has made a feast of thee
> (I, 2).

In the scene where Barnardine the pirate is called to execution, the clown Pompey says :

> He is comming, Sir, he is comming : I heare his straw
> rustle (IV, 3).

And we know that to these beings the whole of life is only a small rat-like rustling in straw, amid a thick and fetid darkness. Claudio, contemplating Death, says :

> To be imprisoned in the viewlesse windes
> And blowne with restlesse violence round about
> The pendant world (III, 1) ;

And we see the world hanging — swinging maybe, like a pendulum, from Man's idea of Good to Man's idea of Evil — over an abyss of Nothingness, or of Hell.

Like doth quit like, and Measure still for Measure,

says the Duke (V, 1). But this is not the only meaning of
the play's title. In this work, all things are weighed against
their apparent opposites — the coldness of virtue against
the cold and calculating sin — the good against the evil in
the heart of Man — the terrors against the peacefulness of
Death — one against the other. The motive and the action,
the good that lies in the one, the sin that lies in the other
— these, too, are weighed.

ISABELLA

Save your Honor !   (*Exeunt*)

ANGELO

From thee ; even from thy vertue !
What's this ? What's this ? Is this her fault, or mine ?
The tempter or the tempted, who sinnes most ?
Ha !
Not she ; nor doth she tempt ; but it is I,
That, lying by the Violet in the Sunne,
Doe as the Carrion do's, not as the flowre,
Corrupt with vertuous season [1] (II, 2).

The play, with its corrupt shreds of flesh that cling about
it, and with the hollow bone devoured by Impiety, seems,
at moments, like the Night wherein the soul is alone with
God. But still the soul hides from itself, though it cannot
hide from God.

The cold and repellent Isabella tells herself that her
natural repulsion against the loathsome attempt of Angelo,
is not a natural repulsion, but a horror of sin as sin. Yet
she does not scruple to lie and cheat. She, herself, acts as
bawd for the very sin for which her brother is to die — and
this, in order to save her own soul !

Claudio had said of Juliet :

You know the lady ; she is fast my wife (I, 2)

---

[1] I find the meaning of this obscure, so add Dr. Johnson's note : ' I am not
corrupted by her, but by my own heart, which excites foul desires under the same
benign influences that exalt her purity, as the carrion grows putrid by those beames
which increase the fragrance of the violet '

and he explains that there is a true contract between them.

Mariana, also, had been troth-plight to Angelo : but whereas Claudio had committed a sin for which he must die, unless respited by mercy, there was, according to Isabella, no sin and no disgrace in what Mariana did — because, apparently, it was expedient.

Towards the end of the play, begging for Angelo's life, in order that he may be given over, an unwilling husband, to Mariana, she says :

> . . . My brother had but justice,
> In that he did the thing for which he di'd.

but, of Angelo,

> His act did not o're take his bad intent ;
> And must be buried but as an intent
> That perish'd by the way.   Thoughts are no subjects ;
> Intents but meerely thoughts (V, 1).

Yet Isabella knows that fault was only not committed, because she had cheated him.   She knew, also, that he, in sending Claudio to his death (for which she seems to care very little), had believed he cheated her — and by a hellish crime.

Isabella knew that Angelo was a hypocrite.   But what was she ?

At least, until the hellish horror of Angelo's final sin (that of ordering the execution of Claudio) — his fall from what he had believed himself to be was, to himself, a tragedy. He even saw himself as he was :

> . . . heaven in my mouth,
> As if I did but onely chew his name,
> And in my heart the strong and swelling evill
> Of my conception (II, 4).

And perhaps that final act which must plunge his soul into Hell was performed in order to cozen himself that though he had betrayed all else, he had not betrayed and broken the letter of the Law of which he was an engine.

He is tragic.   But Isabella is one of the company of the

> Sanctimonious Pyrat, who went to Sea with the Ten Commandments, but scrap'd one out of the Table (I, 2).

'Thrown upon the terrible dilemma of the piece,' says Pater (*Appreciations*), 'called upon to sacrifice that cloistral whiteness to sisterly affection, become in a moment the ground of strong contending passions, she develops a new character and shows herself suddenly of kindred with those strangely conceived women, like Webster's Vittoria, who unite to a seductive sweetness something of a dangerous and tiger-like changefulness of feeling. The swift anger leaps, like a white flame, into this white spirit, and stripped in a moment of all convention, she stands before us, clear, detached, columnar among the tender frailties of the piece.'

Well — no doubt that is how she saw herself — just as the other characters may have seen themselves addicted to ' tender frailties '.

Isabella says to the Duke :

> You bid me seek redemption of the Divell (V, 1).

But, indeed, even goodness seems but the devil in disguise.

In order to obtain possession of an unwilling mate, the forsaken Mariana lends herself to a cheating which is almost as loathsome as Angelo's design upon Mariana — (excepting, of course, that Death was not a pawn in *this* game, and that she thought good — the saving of Claudio's life — would come out of evil).

Not only does the Judge speak with the voice of the tempting devil :

> Might there not be a charity in sinne
> To save thy brother's life ? (II, 4)

but the supposed Man of God (the disguised Duke) in a passage of magnificent poetry, speaks, to the condemned who must die, of Death as if it were only a matter of the cold earth.

> . . . Thou art by no means valiant,
> For thou dost feare the soft and tender forke
> Of a poore worme. Thy best of rest is sleepe,
> And that thou oft provok'st ; yet grossly fear'st
> Thy death, which is no more. . . .

And after speaking of the ills of life :

> . . . What's yet in this,
> That bears the name of life ? Yet in this life
> Lie hid moe thousand deaths : yet death we feare,
> That makes these oddes all even.

But the sinner sees more clearly :

> . . . I humbly thank you.
> To sue to live, I find I seeke to dye —
> And, seeking death, find life (III, 1) :

Yet even in the midst of this filth, the miasma arisen
from the hidden dirt of humanity — in this play where
only the man condemned for sin has an innocent heart,
Shakespeare ' judges not as the judge judges, but as the
sun falling round a helpless thing '.[1]

The Duke, in the speech about Death to which reference
was made earlier, says

> . . . Thou art not noble :
> For all the accommodations that thou bear'st
> Are nurst by basenesse (III, 1).

Of this, Johnson says : ' Whatever grandeur can display,
or luxury enjoy, is procured by *baseness*, by offices of which
the mind shrinks from the contemplation. All the delicacies
of the table may be traced back to the shambles and the
dunghill. All magnificence of building was hewn from the
quarry, and all the pomps of ornament dug from among
the damps of the mine.'

In the same speech, the Duke says :

> . . . Thou art not thy selfe :
> For thou exist'st on many a thousand graines
> That issue out of dust.

[1] Walt Whitman, writing of the poet's nature, in the Preface to *Leaves of Grass*.

We are no better than poor Pompey, to whom the
Duke says :

> Canst thou believe thy living is a life,
> So stinkingly depending ? (III, 2)

We must have mercy upon other dust.   And may there
not be jewels among that dust of which we are made, as
well as the gaudy shining of sin to which Angelo refers ?

> . . . What's open made to Justice,
> That justice ceizes :   What know the Lawes
> That theeves do pass on theeves ?   'Tis very pregnant,
> The jewel that we finde, we stoope and take it
> Because we see it ;   but what we doe not see,
> We tread upon, and never thinke of it (II, 1).

This is the sense that Pater finds in these lines.   As for the
pride of place that has been built upon such dust, while
despising it :

> Respect to your great place !   and let the Divell
> Be some time honour'd for his burning throne (V, 1).

The proud must stoop to see the jewel in the dust.   For
indeed, we are all equally in the need of mercy, as Imogen
says :

> . . . If there be
> Yet left in heaven as small a drop of pitty
> As a wren's eye, fear'd gods, a part of it.
>   (*Cymbeline*, IV, 2)

Instead, Man threatens his own image, in passing judgment.

> Could great men thunder
> As Jove himselfe do's, Jove would nere be quiet,
> For every pelting, petty officer
> Would use his heaven for thunder ;   nothing but thunder.
> Mercifull heaven !
> Thou rather, with thy sharpe and sulphurous bolt
> Splitst the unwedgeable and gnarled oke
> Than the soft Mertill ;   But man, proud man,
> Drest in a little briefe authority,

> Most ignorant of what he's most assur'd —
> His glassie essence — like an angry Ape,
> Playes such phantasticke trickes before high heaven
> As make the Angells weepe ; who, with our spleenes,
> Would all themselves laugh mortall (II, 2).

Says the wicked and heart-corrupted Judge, who had believed himself pure as the heaven :

> It is the law, not I, condemns your brother (II, 2).

The law of Man.   Not the law of God, which is Mercy.

Pompey, no doubt, raised a gale of laughter amid the audience, by his words to Mistress Overdone :

> Courage ! there will be pitty taken on you ; you, that have worne your eies almost out in the service, you will be considered (I, 2).

But there is a great truth, none the less.   She was blind in her sinning.   She and Pompey, like Claudio, had

> . . . but as offended in a dream —

And, no doubt, the heavenly mercy *will* consider blindness, the little or no light, the offence in a dream.   So, in this play in which the brain rebukes the body, coldly, the soul in a blaze of glory speaks to brain and body of pity and redemption, speaks, sometimes, through strange lips.

And as from the lips of Claudio, whose love of life had been too fevered, comes this splendour :

> . . . If I must dye,
> I will encounter darknesse as a bride,
> And hugge it in mine arms (III, 1).

So from the lips of the unconscious hypocrite Isabella — lips cold and perfect as the hailstone, comes this splendour, warm from the heart of heaven :

> . . . alas ! alas !
> Why all the soules that were, were forfeit once ;
> And He that might the vantage best have tooke,

Found out the remedy. How would you be,
If He, which is the top of judgment, should
But judge you as you are ? O ! thinke on that,
And mercy then will breathe within your lips,
Like man new made (II, 2).

Note. The Song

Of this miracle, Swinburne, in *Studies of Shakespeare*,
wrote, ' Shakespeare's verse, as all the world knows, ends
thus :
> But my kisses bring againe,
> Bring againe,
> Seales of love, but seal'd in vaine,
> Seal'd in vaine.

The echo has been dropped by Fletcher, who has thus
achieved the remarkable feat of turning a nightingale's song
into a sparrow's. The mutilation of Philomela by the hands
of Tereus is nothing to the mutilation of Shakespeare by
the hands of Fletcher. . . .'

Part of the poignance of this marvellous song — I
speak of the technical side — is due to the repetition, to
the echoes which sound throughout the verse, and part
to the way in which the imploring stretching outward of
the long vowels in ' Take ' and its internal assonance
' againe ' (and other words with long high vowels) are
succeeded, in nearly every case, in the next stressed foot,
by a word which seems drooping hopelessly, as with ' lips '
and ' forsworne ', for instance.

The third line, however :
> And those eyes, the breake of day,

is an exception. Here, all is hope. Indeed, the sound of
' breake ' and ' day ' rises after the sound of ' eyes '.

A singular beauty, too, is given by the variation in the

length and depth of the pauses. Let us examine the song for a moment :

> Take, oh take those lips away,
> That so sweetly were forsworne ;
> And those eyes, the breake of day,
> Lights that doe mislead the Morne !
> But my kisses bring againe,
> Bring againe,
> Seales of love, but seal'd in vaine,
> Seal'd in vaine.

Note the lightening dissonance of ' lips ' and ' Lights ', the way in which ' breake of day ' would echo, exactly, ' take those lips away ', but for the fact that ' breake ' and ' day ' are drawn more closely together by the space of one syllable. Note, too, the beauty of the assonances ' eyes ' and ' Lights ', and how the particular position in which they are placed gives additional poignancy.

XI

THE FLOWERING DARKNESS: 'ROMEO AND JULIET'

IN all this distillation of the early summer, in which the theme is the same as that of the 65th and 94th Sonnets —

> How with this rage shall beauty hold a plea,
> Whose action is no stronger than a flowre?

and

> The sommer's flowre is to the sommer sweet,
> Though to it selfe it onely live and die —

through the lips of the old Nurse speaks the voice of Nature herself. Almost the tones of Lear are heard (when, for an instant, he blessed the procreation of life before his curse upon it) — but these tones are humble, not royal. And the theme is not of the equality in grandeur of all life, but (disguised beneath those water-chuckling ramblings) it is that of the first two lines in the 1st Sonnet:

> From fairest Creatures we desire increase
> That thereby beautie's Rose might never die.

But

> This bud of love, by Sommer's ripening breath

was never to come to fullness.

Romeo is the brother of the early morning, and as quickly gone —

> With tears augmenting the fresh morning's dew (I, 1),

— inconstant as the morning, inconstant as a dream that is

> Begot of nothing but vaine phantasie;
> Which is as thin of substance as the ayre,
> And more inconstant than the wind, who wooes
> Even now the frozen bosome of the North,

131

> And, being anger'd, puffes away from thence,
> Turning his side to the dew-dropping South (I, 4),

until he saw Juliet.

Throughout the play (with the exception of the Nurse's chatter, and that of the various servants and quarrellers) — all has that miraculous flower-softness, flower-darkness, to which no one but Shakespeare has attained, — the singular beauty which haunts the Sonnets like a perfume.

Old age has ' its vehemence, the effect of spring ', as Coleridge said. But I think rather of the earliest summer.

And the old women with their outworn beauty are like the aged rose, that ' began to put on darknesse, and to decline to softnesse . . . it bowed its stalke, and at Night . . . lost some of its leaves . . .' [1]

The beauty of the lover, enriching Death, becomes a part of the wonder of the universe.

> Come, gentle Night ; come, loving, black-brow'd Night,
> Give me my Romeo : and, when he shall die,
> Take him and cut him out in little starres,
> And he will make the Face of heaven so fine
> That all the world will be in Love with Night,
> And pay no worship to the garish Sun (III, 2).

Romeo, in this work of wonder which is the first of Shakespeare's tragedies, says :

> . . . O my Love ! my wife !
> Death, that hath suck'd the honey of thy breath,
> Hath had no power yet upon thy Beauty :
> Thou art not conquer'd ; Beautie's ensigne yet
> Is Crymson in thy lips and in thy cheekes,
> And Death's pale flag is not advanced there.
>
> .   .   .   .
>
> Why art thou yet so faire ?   Shall I believe
> That unsubstantial Death is amorous,
> And that the leane abhorred Monster keepes
> Thee here in darke to be his Paramour ?

[1] Jeremy Taylor, Sermon.

> For feare of that I still will stay with thee,
> And never from the Palace of dym Night
> Depart againe : here, here will I remaine
> With Wormes that are thy Chambermaides ; O! here
> Will I set up my everlasting rest,
> And shake the yoke of inauspicious starres
> From this world-wearied flesh (V, 3).

When, earlier in the play, he said :

> O ! she doth teach the Torches to burne bright.
> Her Beauty hangs upon the cheeke of night
> Like a rich jewel in an Æthiop's eare (I, 5) ;

was he not seeing her already, without knowing it, as a treasure in the dark night of Death ?

As other commentators have noted, Love is to these young

> Too like the lightning, which doth cease to be
> Ere one can say it lightens (II, 2).

They are the jewels of Death. But the old Nurse is a part of life itself, of the quickening impulse of spring in hedgerow, in nest, in garden wall, — part of the warmth that brings into being the life hidden in insect's egg, in chrysalis.[1]

How different is the magnificence of the later speeches of Romeo, from the sweet flickering shadows — (the years are but these) cast by the summer sun over the quick-running, water-chuckling repetitive talk of the old woman to whom

> Sitting in the sun under the Dove-house wall

the earthquake was no more than the shaking of the dove-house as the doves prepare to fly.

NURSE
> Even or odde, of all daies in the yeare
> Come Lammas Eve at night shall she be fourteene.

. . . .

[1] See Notes on *King Lear*, p. 57.

K

That shall she, marie ; I remember it well.
'Tis since the Earth-quake now eleven yeares ;
And she was wean'd, I never shall forget it,
Of all the daies of the yeare, upon that day ;
For I had then laide worme-wood to my Dugge,
Sitting in the sun under the Dove-house wall ;
My Lord and you were then at Mantua.
Nay, I doe beare a braine : — But, as I said,
When it did taste the worme-wood on the nipple
Of my Dugge and felt it bitter, pretty foole !
To see it tetchie and fall out with the Dugge.
' Shake ' quoth the Dove-house : 'twas no neede, I trow,
To bid mee trudge :
And since that time it is eleven yeares (I, 3) ;

Here, the movement runs as fast as the small shadows over
the grass.   There is but little emphasis, there are but few
hard consonants.   The words ' worme-wood ', ' Dugge ',
' bitter ', ' tetchie ', ' trow ', ' trudge ', delay the movement a
little, are heavier than the rest of the texture.   Otherwise, all
is as soft, as feathered, as the breasts of the doves in the house
beneath which the old woman sits with the baby Juliet.
The running movement is given by the constant use of
double-syllabled words arranged in a particular manner
throughout the lines, and by putting the single-syllabled
words in such places that they are not emphasised, and
consequently move more quickly.

Throughout the whole passage the pauses occur, it
seems, only for want of breath on the part of the speaker.

I have printed the speech as verse, since it appears in
the form of verse in modern editions.   But I am not at all
sure — indeed become less and less sure — that it should
not be printed as prose ; in the Quartos and in the 2nd
and 3rd Folios it is printed as prose.   And I am increasingly
sure that there is much to be said for doing so, since prose
in this particular instance conveys better the pauseless movement, the quickness, the breathlessness of the old woman's
talk.

The verse-beat is not very strong in this passage. In the debatable sleep-walking speeches in *Macbeth* it is very strong — too strong, in my belief, if it were actually to be spoken as verse, for the situation. This leads me to think that in those speeches of Lady Macbeth, Shakespeare meant the beat to underlie, rather than to rule, the sound of the speech, — to be, as it were, a reminder of that Fate-strong will overlaid by sleep, but still, though unconsciously, combating it.

XII

'ANTONY AND CLEOPATRA'

' THE world of *Antony and Cleopatra* ', said Mr. van Doren,[1]
' is so immense that time yawns in it ; and this is not
because time is going to die, as in *Macbeth*, but because it
luxuriates in a sense of perfect and endless health. The
mandragora that Cleopatra wants to drink so that she may
" sleep out the great gap of time " (I, 5) " My Antony is
away ", needs scarcely be drunk in a universe already
drugged with a knowledge of its own size.'

' La musique donne l'idée de l'espace ', said Baudelaire
(*Journaux intimes*), and in the sound of this verse there is the
grandeur of space.

When a Messenger says that a rival conqueror

> . . . hath with his Parthian force
> Extended Asia (I, 2),

— ' extended ', here, means seized. But the word brings
before us all Asia's vastness.

The moments stretch for ever :

> There's not a minute of our lives should stretch
> Without some pleasure now.

says Antony (I, 1).

Kings, drunken with time, with wine, with the noonday
light, nod to each other across a universe of light over
which Antony reigns, like the Sun from which Cleopatra,
the ' day of the world ', takes her light.

. . . .

> . . . Think on me,
> That am with Phoebus' amorous pinches black,
> And wrinckled deepe in time.

[1] *Op. cit.*

136

said Cleopatra (I, 5).   Phoebus : the Sun, who is Antony.
He was all gold — a ' mine of bounty ', with a generosity
like that of the harvest —

> There was no winter in't, an autumn 'twas,
> That grew the more by reaping. . . . (V, 2).

And the mood of this mature conqueror was that of the
time of ripeness :

CLEOPATRA

What ! Was he sad or merry ?

ALEXAS

> Like to the time o' the year between the extremes
> Of hot and cold (I, 5) ;

He

> With his tinct gilded (I, 5)

the messenger who came from him, — like medicinable
gold — or like the autumn sun.

And when Antony says :

> Unarm, Eros ; the long day's task is done,
> And we must sleep (IV, 12),

it is as if the Sun were speaking.

The play has a cosmic splendour, as though the whole
of Nature's ripening Sun had changed, suddenly, to warm
and mellow gold that one can hold in one's hands.

But the Sun sinks, and after his death

> . . . there is nothing left remarkable
> Beneath the visiting moon (IV, 13).

But the darkness is not that of a night haunted by the
Furies and lit by the flares of Hell, but is like the beauty
of one who said :

> . . . Think on me,
> That am with Phoebus' amorous pinches black,
> And wrinckled deep in time.

This night of death, to which the splendours of the day

must sink, the night in which the warrior unarms, his task
done, to find sleep by the side of his lover, is a smiling
darkness.

> Finish, good lady ; the bright day is done,
> And we are for the darke (V, 2).

This softness, this languor, this dark magnificence shapes
the movement, lies on the last scenes like the bloom on
the fruit. Even Death is brought in a basket of figs,
carried by a country clown with the earth about him.

> . . . a rurall Fellow,
> That will not be deny'd your Highnesse' presence :
> He brings you Figges (V, 2).

And lying on all that scene there is this strange and smiling
bloom, the peacefulness of death that is no more fearful
than the shining darkness that lies on the figs.

> CLEOPATRA
>
> Hast thou the pretty Worme of Nylus there,
> That kills and paines not ?
>
> CLOWN
>
> Truly, I have him ; but I would not be the partie
> that should desire you to touch him, for his biting
> is immortal . . .
>
> .   .   .   .   .
>
> . . . I wish you all joy of the Worme (V, 2).

In the slow-moving pomp and splendour of the verse
in the scene of Cleopatra's death, all the vowel-sounds, at
the beginning of the passage, are dark and full, and these
vowels are, in part, the cause of the movement, because
they bring about the pauses :

> CLEOPATRA
>
> Give me my Robe, put on my Crowne ; I have
> Immortall longings in me ; Now no more
> The juyce of Egypt's Grape shall moyst this lip.
> Yare, yare, good Iras ; quicke. Me thinkes I heare

Antony call : I see him rowse himselfe
To praise my noble Act ; I heare him mocke
The lucke of Caesar, which the gods give men
To excuse their after wrath : Husband, I come :
Now to that name my courage prove my Title !
I am Fire and Ayre ; my other elements
I give to baser life. So ; have you done ?
Come then, and take the last warmth of my lippes.
Farewell, kinde Charmian ; Iras, long farewell.
                    (*Kisses them. Iras falls and dies.*)
Have I the Aspicke in my lips ? Dost fall ?
If thou and Nature can so gently part,
The stroke of death is as a Lover's pinch,
Which hurts, and is desir'd. Dost thou lie still ?
If thus thou vanishest, thou tell'st the world
It is not worth leave-taking.

CHARMIAN

Dissolve, thicke Cloud, and Raine ; that I may say
The gods themselves doe weepe.

CLEOPATRA

            This proves me base :
If she first meet the curled Antony,
Hee'l make demand of her, and spend that kisse
Which is my heaven to have. Come, thou mortall wretch,
            (*to the asp, which she places at her breast*)
With thy sharpe teeth this knot intrinsicate
Of life at once untie : Poore venomous Foole,
Be angry, and despatch. O ! couldst thou speake,
That I might heare thee call great Caesar Asse
Unpolicied.

CHARMIAN

O Easterne starre !

CLEOPATRA

            Peace, peace !
Dost thou not see my Baby at my breast,
That suckes the nurse asleepe ?

CHARMIAN

            O breake ! O breake !

CLEOPATRA

As sweet as Balme, as soft as Ayre, as gentle,—
O Antony ! — Nay, I will take thee too.

(*Applying another asp to her arm.*)

What should I stay —   (*Dies.*)

CHARMIAN

In this vile world ? So fare thee well !
Now boast thee, Death, in thy possession lies
A Lasse unparallel'd. Downy Windowes, cloze ;
And golden Phoebus never be beheld
Of eyes again so Royall ! Your Crowne's awry ;
Ile mend it, and then play . . . (V, 2).

In the lines with which Cleopatra's speech begins :

Give me my Robe, put on my Crowne ; I have
Immortall longings in me ; Now no more

— the first line has the same two long dissonantal *o*'s as in
the first line of Lady Macbeth's

And fill me from the Crowne to the Toe, top-full
Of direst Cruelty ! Make thicke my blood (I, 5) ;

— but the place of the dissonances is reversed, and the effect
is utterly different. This is due, in part, to the *t*'s of Lady
Macbeth's lines, and to the *k* and *ck* of ' Make thicke '.
Also, in the second line of Lady Macbeth's, the vowels are
not deep, dark, and rich as are those in the second line of
Cleopatra's in

Give me my Robe, put on my Crowne ; I have . . .

Here the long magnificence of the *o*'s, the first being rich
and deep, but not dark, the second effulgent with brightening jewels — these darken to the splendour of the *o*'s in the
second line — that in ' immortall ' being the deepest ; that
in ' longings ', in spite of the *g* which gives it poignancy,
is soft because of the *n*. The *o* of ' Now ' echoes (though
the length is less) the *o* of ' Crowne ', ' more ' echoes the
' or ' of ' immortall ', and indeed throughout the first lines

there are echoes, some lengthening, some dying away, some more air-thin than the sound of which they are a memory, because of the difference between the consonants that embody the vowels. And these echoes give the verse the miraculous soft balance of the whole.

For instance, 'lucke' in the 7th line is a dulled dissonance to 'quicke' in the 4th and is divided from this by the darker, more hollow dissonance of 'mocke' in the 6th. 'Praise' in the 6th line is a higher dissonantal echo of 'rowse' in the 5th, and 'Come', the first word of the 12th line, is an echo of 'done', the last word in the 11th. In the lines

. . . This proves me base :
If she first meet the curled Antony,
Hee'l make demand of her, and spend that kisse
Which is my heaven to have.

the miraculous balance is due to the dissonances 'base' and 'kisse', and the alliterative *h*'s of 'heaven' and 'have'.

In that wonder of poetry :

CHARMIAN
O Eastern starre !

CLEOPATRA
Peace, peace !
Dost thou not see my Baby at my breast,
That suckes the nurse asleepe ?

CHARMIAN
O breake ! O breake !

CLEOPATRA
As sweet as Balme, as soft as Ayre, as gentle, —

—(the Eastern starre is Venus, the star of the east, and is also Cleopatra, who is all Beauty ; — it is, too, the rising star of death, — all three in one). — The beauty of the sound is due to the balance of the poignant *e*'s of 'Eastern' and 'Peace' — dimming to the *e* of 'breast' — then brightening again, — to the particular arrangement in which the brightening and dimming *e*'s are placed, and, also, to the placing and balancing of the two-syllabled words : the long *e* of ' asleepe ' is a reversed echo of the long *e* of ' Eastern ', the *e* of ' gentle ' is dimmed and softened. The arrangement of *s*'s throughout this passage gives a feeling of strange gentleness, and the fact that they are sometimes placed so that they are alliterative gives balance.

The texture of the passage is for ever darkening and softening, then brightening and becoming poignant once more : ' breast ', for instance, is a higher, slightly dissonantal echo of the dusky, softened ' Dost ', — 'Ayre ' is a softened, bodiless, wavering, dissonantal echo of the shorter, sharper ' starre '.

In the first three lines of that passage which begins with the words ' In this vile world ' there is a lovely pattern of *l*'s, gentle and languorous ; the beauty of the dropping dissonances ' vile ', ' well ' ; ' lies ', ' Lasse ', ' cloze ' is very great.   And it is these, the occasional alliteratives (' world ', ' well ' ; ' lies ', ' Lasse '), the occasional *o*'s, placed close together, of ' Windowes ', ' cloze ', ' golden ', and the perpetual ground-sound (if I may so express it) of *i*'s and *y*'s, —' vile ', ' lies ', ' eyes ', ' awry ' — together with the particular arrangement of assonantal dim *e*'s, — ' well ', ' Death ', ' possession ', ' beheld ', ' mend ', which give the passage its flawless balance.

An extraordinary beauty and strangeness is given in the last four lines of that passage, by the difference in balance and length of the double-syllabled words — the first syllable of ' Downy ' and ' Windowes ' being not quite equal, for the *ow* of 'Downy' is longer, — the first syllables of ' golden ' and ' Phoebus ' being equal, and ' Royall ' being less a word of two syllables than a word of one and three-quarters.

But the whole play is one of the greatest miracles of sound that has ever come into this world.

In the Second Scene of the First Act, for instance, we have this wonder, from the lips of Antony :

> . . . O! then we bring forth weeds
> When our quicke windes lye still! and our illes told us
> Is as our earing. Fare thee well awhile!

Here, the strange beauty is due partly to the change from ' weeds' to ' windes ', from ' still ' to ' illes '.

XIII

'JULIUS CAESAR'

' THE Earth ', said de Quincey, ' has one prerogative City,
and that City was Rome. As was the City, such was its
Prince, — mysterious, solitary, unique. Each was to the
other an adequate counterpart, each reciprocally that perfect
mirror which reflected, as *in alia materia*, those uncommuni-
cable attributes of grandeur that under the same shape and
determination never upon this earth were destined to be re-
vived. Rome has not been repeated : neither has Caesar. . . .
Caesar and Rome have flourished and expired together.
Each, reciprocally, was essential to the other. Even the
Olympian Parthenon needed Rome for its full glorification ;
and Jove himself first knew his own grandeur when robed
and shrined as Jupiter Capitolinus. The illimitable attributes
of the Roman Prince, boundless and comprehensive as the
universal air, — like that also bright and apprehensive to the
most vagrant eye, yet in parts (and those not far removed)
unfathomable as outer darkness (for no chamber could
shroud in more impenetrable concealment a deed of murder
than the chambers of the air) : these attributes, so impressive
to the imagination, and which all the subtlety of the Roman
wit could as little fathom as the fleets of Caesar could
traverse the Polar Basin or unlock the gates of the Pacific,
are best symbolised, and find their most appropriate ex-
ponent, in the illimitable City itself, — that Rome whose
centre, the Capitol, was immovable as Teneriffe or Atlas,
but whose circumference was shadowy, uncertain, restless,
and advancing as the frontiers of her all-conquering
empire.'

As for that empire, ' its range, the compass of its extent,
was appalling to the imagination. Coming last among what

are called the Great Monarchies of Prophecy . . . beyond
it lay Parthia and the great fable of India.' [1]

In this play, the great Caesar, bright as the Prince of the
Powers of the Air, the fallen Angel whose sin was pride,
says, almost at the moment of his death :

I could be well mov'd if I were as you ;
If I could pray to moove, Prayers would moove me ;
But I am constant as the Northerne Starre,
Of whose true fixt and resting quality
There is no fellow in the Firmament.
The skyes are painted with unnumber'd Sparkes,
They are all Fire and every one doth shine :
But there's but one in all doth hold his place :
So in the World.   'Tis furnished well with Men,
And Men are Flesh and Blood, and apprehensive.
Yet in the number I do know but One
That unassayleable holds on to his Ranke,
Unshak'd of Motion : and that I am he (III, 1).

But, in the end, the unshakeable star proved to be Fate, —
a disastrous planet hidden behind the gross mists of the
breath of crowds, — 'the stinking breath' of the crowd
that 'had almost choaked Caesar : for hee swoonded and
fell downe at it' (I, 2).

The voice of Fate sounds not only through the lips of
the Soothsayer who said but five words : ' Beware the Ides
of March ', or amid the strange dream-like mutterings of
the Conspirators in the market-place — one of whom had
seen the swoon of Caesar :

BRUTUS
'Tis very like : he hath the Falling sicknesse.

CASSIUS
No, Caesar hath it not ; but you, and I,
And honest Casca, we have the Falling sicknesse.

CASCA
I know not what you meane by that ; but I am sure
Caesar fell downe. If the tag-ragge people did not

[1] De Quincey, *Philosophy of Roman History.*

clap him, and hisse him, according as he pleas'd and
displeas'd them, as they use to doe the Players in the
theatre, I am no true man (I, 2).

Not these alone, but the Elements, speak of danger :

CASSIUS
              . . . for now, this fearfull Night,
There is no stirre, or walking in the streets ;
And the Complexion of the Element
In Favor's like the Worke we have in hand,
Most bloudie, fierie, and most terrible (I, 3).

                        . . . Never till now,

says Casca,

Did I goe through a tempest dropping fire.

       .   .   .   .   .   .

A common slave — you know him well by sight —
Held up his left hand, which did flame and burne
Like twentie torches joyn'd ; and yet his Hand,
Not sensible of fire, remain'd unscorch'd.
Besides, — I have not since put up my sword, —
Against the Capitoll I met a Lyon,
Who glar'd upon me, and went surly by (I, 3).

Calpurnia says to Caesar :

A lioness hath whelped in the streets (II, 2) ;

— and this seems like the birth of Disaster, or of some
terrible new-fallen Angel — half lion, half spirit, fallen
before his birth. But Caesar does not heed the complexion
of the elements. He remains deaf to the dream of his wife,
as to the voice of the Soothsayer :

CAESAR
                    What say the augurers ?

SERVANT
They would not have you to stirre forth to-day.
Plucking the intrailes of an offering forth,
They could not finde a heart within the beast.

CAESAR

The Gods do this in shame of Cowardice :
Caesar should be a Beast without a heart
If he should stay at home to-day for feare.
No, Caesar shall not ; Danger knowes full well
That Caesar is more dangerous than he :
We are two Lyons litter'd in one day,
And I the elder and more terrible (II, 2).

Even Voltaire, in the midst of his cavilling, was moved to exclaim that this is of an inconceivable elevation.

The play is amongst the most *pure* poetry written by Shakespeare. The theme is the greatness of Man pitted against the power of Fate. The poetry itself has the complexion of the elements. It moves with an incredible grandeur, as it tells of the bright Angel Caesar — the Angel, perhaps, of Death, who must fall from his place as Lucifer fell, because of pride, or because of the pride that his killers believed existed in him.

BRUTUS

It must be by his death : and, for my part,
I know no personall cause to spurne at him,
But for the generall. He would be crowned :
How that might change his nature, there's the question :
It is the bright day that brings forth the adder ;
And that craves warie walking. Crowne him ? — that !
And then, I graunt, we put a Sting in him.
That at his will he may doe danger with.
The abuse of Greatnesse is, when it dis-joynes
Remorse from Power (II, 1).

There is a strange beauty in this scene, when Brutus, returning from his orchard to the closet, says :

The exhalations whizzing in the Ayre
Give so much light that I may reade by them (II, 1).

A few moments later, comes the knock on the door. It is the knock of Fate. From that moment, there is only one road on which Brutus may travel.

This knocking on the door is only one of the several incidents which, as various commentators have pointed out, connect the play with *Macbeth*.

In *Julius Caesar*, however, the knocking foretold the deed. It did not, as in *Macbeth*, tell that the deed was done, and that the gates of Hell would soon close behind the doer.

Brutus, hearing of the death of his beloved wife Portia, says :

> Speake no more of her (IV, 3).

And, mourning over the death of Cassius :

> Friends, I owe more teares
> To this dead man than you shall see me pay.
> I shall find time, Cassius : I shall find time (V, 3).

Both these passages seem like forerunners of that wherein Macbeth hears of the death of his wife.

Then, too, there is the scene where the Ghost of Caesar confronts Brutus, and the living man says :

> How ill this Taper burns !   Ha ! who comes heere ?
> I thinke it is the weaknesse of mine eyes
> That shapes this monstrous Apparition.
> It comes upon me.   Art thou any thing ?
> Art thou some God, some Angell, or some Divell,
> That makst my blood cold, and my haire to stare ?
> Speake to me what thou art.

GHOST

Thy evill Spirit, Brutus.

BRUTUS

Why com'st thou ?

GHOST

To tell thee thou shalt see me at Philippi.

BRUTUS

Well : then I shall see thee againe ?

GHOST

Ay, at Philippi.

BRUTUS

Why, I will see thee at Philippi then (IV, 3).

The beginning recalls the moment when Macbeth sees the Ghost of Banquo. But to his questioning, that Ghost made no answer. The Ghost of Caesar speaks with the dark voice of an Augury.

The end of the play contains two supreme grandeurs :

TITINIUS

But Cassius is no more. O setting Sunne !
As in thy red Rayes thou dost sinke to night,
So in his red blood Cassius' day is set ;
The Sunne of Rome is set. Our day is gone ;
Cloudes, Dewes, and Dangers come : our deeds are done
(V, 3).

And Brutus :

Night hangs upon mine eyes ; my Bones would rest,
That have but labour'd to attaine this houre (V, 5).

.   .   .   .   .   .

' With polysyllabic and ample-sounding words ' (to paraphrase a sentence by Gautier), ' verses are made which seem immense, and in which these vibrating sounds prolong the measure.'

And here, in *Julius Caesar*, are words whose vibrating sounds prolong the measure. But they are more often words of one syllable than polysyllabic. The voices sound, often, with the resonance of dark marbles, of bronze, of porphyry.

L

XIV

'TITUS ANDRONICUS'

' THE true lyon knoweth, sayth Pliny, when the lyonnesse
hath played him false play, and hath played the advoutresse
with the libard, by a certain rammish smell or sweate which
ariseth from them both.' [1]

Certainly in this case there has been an advoutrie with
the libard, and yet — rammish smell or no rammish smell,
there are dark and turgid, earthy splendours that could
come from one hand alone.

> When did the Tiger's young ones teach the dam ?
> O ! doe not learne her wrath ; she taught it thee ;
> The milke thou suck'st from her did turn to Marble ;
> Even at thy Teat thou hadst thy Tyranny (II, 3).

This, I think, is brother to certain lines in *King Lear*.
Speaking of his grief, Titus says (III, 1) :

> What foole hath added water to the Sea,
> Or brought a faggot to bright burning Troy ?
> My griefe was at the height before thou cam'st ;

In the Fourth Scene of the Fourth Act comes this
grandeur :

TAMIRA

> King, be thy thoughts imperious like thy name.
> Is the Sunne dim'd, that Gnats doe flye in it ?
> The Eagle suffers little Birds to sing,
> And is not carefull what they meane thereby,
> Knowing that with the shadow of his wings
> He can at pleasure stint their melody ;
> Even so mayst thou the giddy men of Rome.

---

[1] '*The Greene Forest, or a Naturale historie*, compiled by John Maplet, M. of Arte,
Student in Cambridge, entending hereby that God might especially be glorified,
and the people furdered. London, 1567.'

The scene (IV, 3) in which a clown enters with a basket and two pigeons in it, seems like a lesser forerunner of the strange scene in which a clown brings Death to Cleopatra in a basket of figs.

XV

TWO NOTES ON 'TROILUS AND CRESSIDA'

Note I

' THE Doctrine of Order ', as Dr. E. M. W. Tillyard points out, runs through the plays of Shakespeare. See the Historical Tragedies, *The Tempest*. It is implicit in the speech of Ulysses to Agamemnon :

> When that the Generall is not like the Hive,
> To whom the Forragers shall all repaire,
> What Hony is expected ? Degree being vizarded,
> The unworthiest shewes as fairely in the Maske.
> The Heavens themselves, the Planets, and this Centre
> Observe degree, priority, and place,
> Insisture, course, proportion, season, forme,
> Office and custome, in all line of Order :
> And therefore is the glorious Planet Sol
> In noble eminence enthron'd and sphear'd
> Amidst the other : whose med'cinable eye
> Corrects the ill Aspects of Planets evill,
> And posts, like the Commandment of a King,
> Sans checke, to good and bad : but when the Planets
> In evill mixture to disorder wander,
> What Plagues, and what Portents, what mutiny,
> What raging of the Sea, shaking of Earth,
> Commotion in the Windes, Frights, Changes, Horrors,
> Divert and cracke, rend and deracinate
> The unity and married calme of States
> Quite from their fixure ! O ! when degree is shak'd,
> Which is the Ladder to all high designes,
> The enterprise is sicke. How could Communities,
> Degrees in Schooles, and brother-hoods in Cities,
> Peacefull Commerce from dividable shores,
> The primogenitive and due of Byrth,
> Prerogative of Age, Crownes, Sceptres, Laurels,
> But by degree, stand in Authentique place ?

Take but degree away, untune that string,
And, hark! what Discord follows ; each thing meets
In meere oppugnancy : the bounded Waters
Should lift their bosomes higher than the Shores
And make a soppe of all this solid globe :

. . . . . .

Then every thing includes it selfe in Power,
Power into Will, Will into Appetite ;
And Appetite, a universall Wolfe,
So doubly seconded with Will and Power,
Must make perforce a universall prey,
And last, eat up himselfe. Great Agamemnon,
This Chaos, when degree is suffocate,
Followes the choaking.   (*Troilus and Cressida*, I, 3)

Dr. Tillyard, in *Shakespeare's History Plays*, quotes from
' the original book of Homilies published in 1547 when
Edward VI was King'. The passage comes from the
opening of the *Sermon of Obedience, or An Exhortation concerning good Ordre and Obedience to Rulers and Magistrates*.

' Almightie God hath created and appoynted all thynges,
in heaven, yearth, and waters, in a most excellent and perfect
ordre. In heaven he hath appoynted distincte Orders and
states of Archangelles and Angelles. In the yearth he hath
assigned Kynges, princes, and other governors under them,
all in good and necessarie ordre. The water above is kepte
and raineth downe in dewe time and season. The Sonne,
Moone, Sterres, Rainbowe, Thundre, Lightenyng, Cloudes,
and all birds of the aire, do kepe their ordre. The yearth,
Trees, Seedes, Plantes, Herbes, and Corne, Grasse, and all
maner of beastes kepe them in their ordre. All the partes
of the whole yere, as Winter, Somer, Moneths, Nightes and
Daies, continue in their ordre. All kyndes of Fishes in the
sea, Rivers and Waters, with all Fountaines, Sprynges, yea,
the Seas themselves kepe their comely course and ordre.
And Man himselfe, also, hath all his partes, both within
and without, as Soule, Harte, Mynde, Memory, Understanding, Reason, Speache, with all and syngular corporall

membres of his body in a profitable necessarie and pleasaunt ordre. Euery degree of people, in their vocacion, callyng, and office, hath appointed to them their duetie and ordre. Some are in high, some in lowe, some Kynges and Princes, some inferiors and subjectes, Priestes and Laymen, Masters and Servauntes, Fathers and Children, Husbandes and Wifes, Riche and Poore, and euery one hath nede of other, so that in all thynges is to bee lauded and praised the goodly ordre of God, without the whiche, no house, no citie, no common wealthe, can continue and endure. For where there is no right ordre, there reigneth all abuse, carnall libertie, enormitie, synne, and Babylonicall confusion. Take awaie Kynges, Princes, Rulers, Magistrates, Judges, and such states of God's ordre, no man shall ride or go by the high way unrobbed, no man shall slepe in his owne house or bed unkilled, no man shall kepe his wife, children, and possessions in quietnesse, all thynges shall be common, and there must nedes folowe all mischief and utter destruccion, bothe of soules, bodies, goodes, and common wealthes.'

Dr. Tillyard says : ' This passage and Ulysses' speech are close enough together to make it likely that at least an unconscious act of memory took place. It is also possible that it was first through this homily that Shakespeare had that idea of degree impressed on his mind.'

In *Troilus and Cressida*, the low is ever seeking to pull down the high.

Among these beings, like ' the appearances which spring up in sleep or by day, such as a shadow when darkness arises in a fire ' [1] — among the heroes of an airy brightness and splendour — (of Hector, Ulysses says :

> His crest that prouder than blue Iris bends)

walks the horrible Thersites, the smaller embodiment of a general Chaos, casting

> . . . the dry serpigo on the subject.

[1] Plato, quoted by Burton, *The Anatomy of Melancholy*.

He takes and ruins all great sentences. He seems the breath of the crowd on the immovably centred hero.

Nestor, the old wise being who sees

> The baby figure of the gyant-masse
> Of things to come at large,

says (I, 3):

> Tell him of Nestor, one that was a man
> When Hector's Grandsire suck't : he is old now :
> But if there be not in our Grecian host
> One noble man that hath one sparke of fire
> To answer for his Love, tell him from me,
> I'll hide my Silver beard in a Gold Beaver,
> And in my Vantbrace put this wither'd brawne ;
> And meeting him, will tell him that my lady
> Was fairer than his Grandam, and as chaste
> As may be in the world : His youth in flood,
> I'll prove this truth with my three drops of blood.

This speech of old age has the grandeur and serenity of a golden afternoon.

Thersites was not present, but in the next scene (II, 1) he speaks as if the high and noble air had stirred his base dust to a baser echo :

> There's Ulysses and old Nestor, whose wit was mouldy
> ere your grandsires had nails on their toes. . . .

Note II

Some lines of this play have the soft and smiling loveliness of Marlowe :

> I stalk about her door
> Like a strange soul upon the Stygian banks
> Staying for waftage (III, 2).

Here, the lovely sound is due to the differing *a*'s and the lengthening *s*'s, with their different heights.

XVI

'TROILUS AND CRESSIDA', 'THE HENRIAD', SHAKESPEARE AND MARLOWE

THE Sun borrows of the moon when Diomed keepes his word,

said the evil Thersites (V, 1). And though that particular magnificence, and many others, seem, to one reader at least, to be Shakespeare's, there are passages in this play in which either the sun Shakespeare has borrowed of the moon Marlowe, or else the moon rules.

Often the beauties of the play have a soft and smiling nature reminiscent of Marlowe in certain moods. There are, however, passages in Marlowe in which there is no softness.

The play has been held by certain critics to be by Marlowe because of a similitude between the play's imagery and Marlowe's.

But we do not tell the work of a poet so much by the use of imagery (unless the imagery is exceedingly unusual) as by something inimitable in the gait. The late J. M. Robertson, chief sceptic (*Shakespeare Canon*, Part IV, Division II), admits that. And if a similitude of imagery is the proof of a poet's identity, then we must assume that Marlowe, who wrote (*Triumphs of Tamburlaine*, II, 1)

> And when his princely Persean Diadem
> Shall overway his wearie witlesse head,
> And fall like mellowed fruit, with shakes of death

— wrote also

> Ripenesse is all.

There are, however, phrases which seem to be Shakespeare's alone, when bearing a certain meaning. In nearly all cases when he uses the word 'water-drops' he means tears. As in the Second Scene of the Third Act of *Troilus and Cressida* :

> If I be false, or swerve a haire from truth,
> When time is old and hath forgot it selfe,
> When water-drops have worn the stones of Troy,
> And blinde oblivion swallow'd Cities up,
> And mightie States characterlesse are grated
> To dustie nothing, yet let memory,
> From false to false, among false Maids in love
> Upbraid my falsehood. . . .

Or again, as in *King Richard II* (IV, 1),

> O that I were a Mockerie King of Snow,
> Standing before the Sunne of Bolingbroke,
> To melt myself away in Water-drops !

In the last passage, the movement *does* bear a certain resemblance to that of Marlowe. Even so, it might be the movement of another great poet.

Marlowe is usually unmistakable. He has a walk like that of no other poet. He treads the air like the Dauphin's palfrey : ' He is pure Ayre and Fire ; and the dull elements of Earth and Water never appear in him, but only in patient stilnesse '.

None but he seems such a fire in the air. A bird sang in his voice.

One of the signs of Marlowe at his greatest, is the *upward* movement with which each line ends. This ending is not, of course, invariable, for that would be monotonous. It does not apply to the ineffable lines about Helen, or the last lines of *Faustus*. . . . But it is a sign and a portent in *Tamburlaine*. There, each line, in passage after passage, seems to soar into the air. Elsewhere, the line ends with an extraordinary crispness.

One of the unmistakable, inimitable signs of Shakespeare, in certain lines, is his ' dying fall '.

Mr. J. M. Robertson cites lines which *could* not have been by Marlowe, — could not, by the very manner of their gait, — as his, because of their imagery.

In the *Shakespeare Canon*, Part IV, Division II, he compares this speech of York's (*King Henry the Sixth*, Part II, V, 3),

> Of Salisbury, who can report of him,
> That winter Lyon, who in rage forgets
> Aged contusions and all brush of Time,
> And like a Gallant in the brow of youth
> Repaires him with Occasion,

and these lines of Techelles (*The Conquests of Tamburlaine*, I, 2),

> As princely lions when they rouse themselves,
> Stretching their pawes, and threatening heardes of Beasts,
> So in his armour looketh Tamburlaine.

He deduces from the lion image, that York's lines may be by Marlowe. I cannot conceive why. The comparison of a lion with a hero is surely one that might be, and has been, made by a thousand writers. The *movement* of the two passages is entirely different.

. . . .

All the characters in Marlowe, excepting Faustus at the moment of his damnation, when he speaks with the agony of a great human soul — are glories of the air, and not beings of the earth in whose hearts the pulses of the spring and of the earth beat. Their gait is a planetary movement — as splendid and as uncaring.

But in this passage from *King Henry the Sixth*, the great heart of Shakespeare feels for the bravery of the old lion.

Again Mr. Robertson, referring to these lines from the Second Part of *King Henry the Sixth*,

> Ah, barbarous villaines ! Hath this lovely face
> Ruled, like a wandering Plannet, over me,
> And could it not inforce them to relent,
> That were unworthy to behold the same ? (IV, 4)

says, ' it is, perhaps, only the poverty of " the same " that would dissuade idolatry from giving the second line to Shakespeare '.

He points out, however, in a footnote, that ' Ruled, like
a wandering Plannet, over me ' is Marlowe's — because
Marlowe often applied the adjective ' wandering ' to a
planet, — although he adds : ' Of course, both items are
to be found elsewhere ; but the whole form here is his,
unless he is being carefully imitated '. I would have thought
that ' a wandering Plannet ' lay in every man's possession.
But there are reasons why we may believe that this line,
which is of such a beauty that it is worthy of the planet's
heaven, may have been Marlowe's. It moves with a perfection of softness which is particularly his, and which
appears in :

> When wandering Phoebe's Ivory cheeks were scorch't,
> And all the earth like Ætna breathing fire
>
> (*Tamburlaine*, II)

— where, again, the adjective ' wandering ' is used. And

> O thou art fairer than the evening aire,
> Clad in the beauty of a thousand starres ;
> Brighter art thou than flaming Jupiter.

Perhaps, indeed, such lines as

> And cause the stars fixt in the Southern Arke
> Whose lovely faces never any viewed

might have led to this passage in *King Henry the Sixth*.
The lines in *King Henry the Sixth*, calling on the comets
to

> Brandish your crystall tresses in the sky,
> And with them scourge the bad revolting Stars
> That have consented unto Henrie's death!

— these were enough, says Mr. Robertson, to convince
Swinburne that the play was Marlowe's own. ' They at
once recall the line

> That shone as comets menacing revenge.'
>
> (*Tamburlaine*, III, 2)

There I agree.

He adds that

> Brandish your crystall tresses in the sky

points straight to

> Flora in her morning's pride
> Shaking her siluer tresshes in the air
>
> (*Tamburlaine*, I, v, 2)

and

> My horsemen *brandish* their unruly blades.

The example of the ' unruly blades ' seems really too far-fetched.

Mr. Robertson declares that ' crystal was one of Marlowe's frequent meteorological epithets ' : and I cannot but agree with him that the entire theme, the strong but simple rhythm, the diction, the imagery, would seem to be Marlowe's.

Coleridge (*Lectures*, 1818, Section 3) wrote : ' Read aloud any two or three passages in blank verse even from Shakespeare's earliest dramas, as *Love's Labour's Lost* or *Romeo and Juliet*, and then read in the same way this speech, with especial attention to the metre ; and if you do not feel the impossibility of the latter having been written by Shakespeare all I dare suggest is, that you may have ears, for so has another animal, — but an ear you cannot have, *me judice* '.

Mr. Robertson would certainly seem to have made his point about this passage. At other times, however, he was less fortunate, — as when, for instance, he ascribed to Kyd the part of *King Henry the Sixth* containing the line

> Dazzle mine eyes, or do I see three suns ?

This, he declares, points to a line in Kyd's *Soliman and Perseda* (II, 1),

> Dazzle mine eyes, or is't Lucina's chain ?

He might really almost as well say that Webster's

> Cover her up : mine eyes dazzle. She died young

was written by Kyd !

XVII

NOTE ON THE HISTORICAL TRAGEDIES

. . . THE histories of our English kings — the events of their reigns, I mean, — are like stars in the sky; whatever the real interspaces may be, and however great, they seem close to each other. The stars — the events — strike us and remain in our eyes little modified by the difference of dates.—S. T. COLERIDGE.

XVIII

SOME GENERAL NOTES ON THE TRAGEDIES RELATING TO THE ENGLISH KINGS

It will have blood, they say : Blood will have Blood.

(Macbeth, III, 4)

AND in these works, wherein War and Death come, like over-lords, to walk among their tributary Kings,[1] one theme is a guilt that is like that of the Atridae.

Plantagenet doth quit Plantagenet.

(King Richard the Third, IV, 4)

And of Edward the Third's sons, the widow of one cried to his brother Gaunt :

> Edward's seven sonnes, whereof thyselfe art one,
> Were as seven vialles of his sacred blood,
> Or seven faire branches springing from one roote :
> Some of those seven are dry'd by Nature's course,
> Some of those branches by the Destinies cut ;
> But Thomas, my deere Lord, my life, my Gloucester,
> One viall full of Edward's sacred blood,
> One flourishing branch of his most Royall roote,
> Is crack'd, and all the precious liquor spilt,
> Is hack't downe, and his summer leaves all faded
> By Envy's hand . . .

(King Richard the Second, I, 2)

Blood is the triumphant arch through which the murdering

[1] ' Ha, Majesty ! how high thy glory towres,
When the rich blood of Kings is set on fire ! '

(King John, II, 1)

'. . . For within the hollow Crowne
That roundes the mortall Temples of a King
Keepes Death his Court, and there the Antique sits
Scoffing his State and grinning at his pompe,
Allowing him a breath, a little Scene,
To Monarchize, be fear'd and kill with lookes.'

(King Richard the Second, III, 2)

Kings pass to their kingdom. Blood is the beggar sitting by the roadside, waiting to beg of their majesty.[1]

In each of these plays there is a sacrificial victim — young and beautiful : Arthur, to whom his mother said :

> Of Nature's gifts thou mayst with Lillies boast
> And with the halfe blowne Rose.
>
> (*King John*, III, 1)

— Richard the Second, the youthful Clarence, the two young Princes, sons of Richard the Fourth.

But Death is just, and loves the beauty it has taken. The young shade of a murdered boy has the beauty of light — is

> A shadow like an Angell, with bright haire.
>
> (*King Richard the Third*, I, 4)

Grief and deprivation have the purity of snow, and its light :

> O that I were a Mockery King of Snow,
> Standing before the Sunne of Bolingbroke
> To melt my selfe away in water-drops !

says Richard the Second (IV, 1).

Grief fills the heart with an exquisite tenderness — fills the place of the lost one : from the lips of Constance, who had been called an ' unadvised scold ', comes this ineffable shadowed music :

> And, father Cardinall, I have heard you say
> That we shall see and know our friends in heaven :
> If that be true, I shall see my boy againe ;
> For since the birth of Caine, the first male child,
> To him that did but yesterday suspire
> There was not such a gracious creature borne.
> But now will canker sorrow eate my bud
> And chase the native beauty from his cheeke
> And he will looke as hollow as a Ghost,
> As dim and meagre as an Ague's fit,
> And so hee'll dye ; and, rising so againe,

---

[1] ' English Seneca read by candlelight yeeldes many good sentences, as Bloud is a beggar.'— Nash's Preface to Greene's *Menaphon*.

When I shall meet him in the Court of heaven
I shall not know him : therefore never, never
Must I behold my pretty Arthur more.

. . . . . .

KING PHILIP
You are as fond of griefe as of your child.

CONSTANCE
Griefe fills the roome up of my absent child,
Lies in his bed, walkes up and down with me,
Puts on his pretty lookes, repeates his words,
Remembers me of all his gracious parts,
Stuffes out his vacant garments with his forme.
Then have I reason to be fond of griefe.
Fare you well : had you such a losse as I,
I could give better comfort than you doe.
(*King John*, III, 4)

The child whose foster-brother was Grief, must go to

His little kingdome of a forcèd grave,
(*King John*, IV, 2)

but he who took the child's heritage of another kingdom
was not to enjoy it.

The tyrant was King, but the Light is a yet greater king
— and that, in conjunction with the common humanity of
the flesh, would seem to him, at first, to defeat him.

I had a thing to say, but let it goe :
The Sunne is in the heaven, and the proud day,
Attended with the pleasures of the world,
Is all too wanton and too full of gawdes
To give me audience : if the midnight bell
Did, with his iron tongue and brazen mouth,
Sound on into the drowzy ear of night ;
If this same were a Church-yard where we stand,
And thou possessed with a thousand wrongs ;
Or if that surly spirit, melancholy,
Had bak'd thy bloud and made it heavy, thicke,
Which else runnes tickling up and downe the veines,
Making that idiot, laughter, keepe men's eyes

And straine their cheekes to idle merriment,
A passion hatefull to my purposes ;
Or if that thou couldst see me without eyes,
Heare me without thine eares, and make reply
Without a tongue, using conceit alone,
Without eyes, eares and harmefull sound of words ;
Then, in despite of broad-eyed watchfull day,
I would into thy bosome poure my thoughts :
But, ah, I will not ! yet I love thee well ;
And, by my troth, I thinke thou lov'st me well.

HUBERT

So well, that what you bid me undertake,
Though that my death were adjunct to my Act,
By heaven, I would doe it.

KING JOHN

Doe not I know thou wouldst ?
Good Hubert, Hubert, Hubert, throw thine eye
On yon young boy : Ile tell thee what, my friend,
He is a very serpent in my way ;
And wheresoe'er this foot of mine doth tread,
He lyes before me : dost thou understand me ?
Thou art his keeper.

HUBERT

And Ile keepe him so,
That he shall not offend your Majesty.

KING JOHN

Death.

HUBERT

My Lord ?

KING JOHN

A Grave.

HUBERT

He shall not live.

KING JOHN

Enough.
I could be merry now. Hubert, I love thee (III, 3) ;

M

Throughout this great passage, the constantly recurring *s*'s hiss like a serpent. In the lines :

> I had a thing to say, but let it goe :
> The Sunne is in the heaven, and the proud day,

— the rhymes (internal and external) rear themselves up, like a serpent about to strike.

At other times, these *s*-weighted words slide or drag along, as if they were hiding from the light of day — with the movements of a serpent, of

> ' Scorpion and Asp, and Amphisbæna dire,
> Cerastes horned, Hydras, and Ellops drear.' [1]

The common humanity of eyes and ears defeated the King of his purpose, and the child went to his ' little kingdome ' through a mischance.

In one of those prophetic speeches uttered by lips that knew not their full meaning — those strange mutterings and foreshadowings of doom that occur in Shakespeare's works, King John and the King of France speak thus :

KING JOHN

> France, I am burn'd up with inflaming wrath ;
> A rage whose heat hath this condition,
> That nothing can allay, nothing but blood,
> The blood, and deerest-valued blood, of France.

KING PHILIP

> Thy rage shall burne thee up, and thou shalt turne
> To ashes, ere our blood ahall quench that fire :
> Look to thy selfe, thou art in jeopardy (III, 1).

In the end, poison does that which hatred might have done. The King says :

> There is so hot a Summer in my bosome,
> That all my bowels crumble up to dust :
> I am a scrabbled forme, drawne with a pen
> Upon a Parchment, and against this fire
> Doe I shrinke up.

[1] *Paradise Lost.*

PRINCE HENRY

How fares your Majestie ?

KING JOHN

Poisoned — ill fare — dead, forsooke, cast off :
And none of you will bid the Winter come
To thrust his ycie fingers in my maw,
Nor let my Kingdome's Rivers take their course
Through my burn'd bosome, nor intreat the North
To make his bleake windes kisse my parched lips
And comfort me with cold. I doe not aske you much,
I beg cold comfort ; and you are so strait
And so ingratefull, you deny me that.

PRINCE HENRY

O that there were some vertue in my teares
That might relieve you.

KING JOHN

The salt in them is hot.
Within me is a hell ; and there the poison
Is as a fiend, confined to tyrannize
On unreprievable condemnèd blood (V, 7).

.   .   .   .   .

I am a scrabbled forme, drawne with a pen
Upon a Parchment, and against this fire
Doe I shrinke up.

He saw himself, perhaps, as the parchment on which he had
written the order to blind the child Arthur, — a parchment
burning now, for ever, in the fire of Hell.

Within me is a hell.

It was self-bred, self-engendered. And the fires of the
Monk's poison had come to join that greater Hell.

.   .   .   .   .   .

Amongst these untamed and ravening beasts, the nobles,
and the yet more ferocious tyrant-kings —

Beauty is no stronger than a flowre.

Of the *Henriad*, Pater wrote : ' as in a children's story,

all Princes are in extremes. Delightful in the sunshine above a wall into which chance lifts the flower for a season, they can but plead somewhat more touchingly than others their everyday weakness in the storm.'

This is even more true of Richard the Second :

> The King Richard of Yngland
> Was in his flouris then regnand :
> But his flouris efter sone
> Fadyt and ware all undone

said the Chronicle.[1]

'It is this irony of kingship' (said Pater), 'the sense that it is in its happiness child's play, and in its sorrows, after all, child's grief, which gives the finest accent to all the changeful feelings of the wonderful speeches : the great meekness of the graceful wild creature, tamed at last :

> Give Richard leave to live till Richard die.'[2]

But

> O that I were as great
> As is my grief

— says the flower about to fall (III, 3).

> NORTHUMBERLAND
> . . . May it please you to come downe ?

> KING RICHARD
> Downe, downe I come ; like glist'ring Phaethon,
> Wanting the manage of unruly jades (III, 3).

So, before the great Ritual of Darkness which is to take place in *King Richard the Third*, there is the Ritual of the Falling of the Sun. Richard, made great by grief, appears now, no longer as the flower that is the small-rayed simulacrum of the Sun, but as the Sun himself. And this ritual has all the slow magnificence of the Sun as it falls.

.   .   .   .   .   .

---

[1] Quoted by Pater, *Appreciations.*
[2] Pater, *op. cit.*

Yet, when that reversal has taken place, the King who is no higher than the earth from which he was made can say,

> . . . still my Griefes are mine :
> You may my Glories and my State depose,
> But not my Griefes ; still am I King of those (IV, 1).

. . . . . .

Behind the murdering or murdered Kings, stand the Queens and Princesses, wife or mother, like Fates, like Furies, or like fountains of tears.

In *The Life and Death of King John*, there is

> . . . the mother-queen,
> An Ate, stirring him to blood and strife (II, 1).

But the terrible Queen Margaret overshadows her.

'. . . Just as the blood of Dido, the Carthaginian queen' (said De Quincey), 'after mounting to the heavens, under her dying imprecation,

> Exoriare aliquis nostris ex ossibus ultor,

came round in a vast arch of bloodshed upon Rome, under the retaliation of Hannibal, four or five centuries later', — so it is with the blood of the slain Plantagenet Kings and Princes, with the appalling curses of Margaret, with the curse of her enemy York.

But Grief is of the company of Kings, and before Grief all must bow. Only the noble earth is worthy to be Grief's throne.

> I will instruct my sorrowes to be proud ;
> For Greif is proud and makes his owner stoope.
> To me and to the state of my great griefe
> Let Kings assemble ; for my Greif's so great
> That no supporter but the huge firme earth
> Can hold it up : here I and sorrowes sit ;
> Here is my Throne, bid Kings come bow to it.

And Constance seats herself upon the ground (*King John*, III, 1).

Grief puts into the mouth of that Ate Margaret, that phrase of a melting beauty, quoted in another passage :

> Ah, barbarous villaines !   Hath this lovely face
> Ruled, like a wandering Plannet, over me,
> And could it not inforce them to relent,
>
> (*King Henry the Sixth*, Part II, IV, 4)

And after the final desolation has come upon her, though she is now metamorphosed from the epitome of all beauty into a

> Foule wrinckled witch

— and though hatred still burns in her veins like fire, the queenship of her grief makes her seek the company of the Queens whom she had cursed, the royal Duchess upon whom she had brought disaster, and by whose sons, in turn, disaster had fallen upon her.   She joins them as if they must take part together in some great Ceremonial.   Her sorrows, her hatred, have brought upon them their doom :   their sorrows have condemned her.   Railing and hating, she had called upon them the curse of Heaven, and it had fallen upon them.   But the shadow thrown across the light of the Sun by the raising of Richard the Third's withered arm, changed to a universal darkness.   And under that darkness she too was buried.   Curser and cursed were equal then.

QUEEN MARGARET

> If ancient sorrow be most reverend,
> Give mine the benefit of signeury,
> And let my Greefes frowne on the upper hand.
>
> (*Sitting down with them*)
>
> If sorrow can admit Society,
> Tell o'er your woes again by viewing mine :
> I had an Edward, till a Richard kill'd him :
> I had a Harry, till a Richard kill'd him :
> Thou hadst an Edward, till a Richard kill'd him.
> Thou hadst a Richard, till a Richard kill'd him.

DUCHESS

> I had a Richard too, and thou didst kill him.
> I had a Rutland too, thou holpst to kill him.

QUEEN MARGARET

Thou hadst a Clarence, too, and Richard kill'd him.
From forth the kennell of thy wombe hath crept
A Hell-hound that doth hunt us all to death :
That Dogge that had his teeth before his eyes,
To worry Lambes and lap their gentle blood,
That foule defacer of God's handy worke,
That excellent grand Tyrant of the earthe,
That reignes in gauled eyes of weeping soules,
Thy wombe let loose to chase us to our graves.
O upright, just, and true-disposing God,
How do I thank thee, that this carnall Curre
Preyes on the issue of his Mother's body,
And makes her Pue-fellow with others' mone.

DUCHESS

O Harrie's wife, triumph not in my woes !
God witnesse with me, I have wept for thine.

QUEEN MARGARET

Beare with me ; I am hungry for revenge,
And now I cloy me with beholding it.
Thy Edward he is dead, that stabb'd my Edward ;
Thy other Edward dead, to quit my Edward ;
Young Yorke he is but boote, because both they
Match not the high perfection of my losse.
Thy Clarence he is dead, that kill'd my Edward ;
And the beholders of this franticke play,
Th' adulterate Hastings, Rivers, Vaughan, Grey,
Untimely smother'd in their dusky graves.

(*King Richard the Third*, IV, 4)

.   .   .   .   .   .

Of this great paean to the power of Death, Dr. Tillyard has
already noted that the incantation takes the form not only
of an obvious antiphony like Queen Margaret's balancing
of her own woes with Queen Elizabeth's . . . but of a
more complicated balance of rhythmic phrases and of
varied repetitions, as in the Duchess of York's self-address :

Blind sight, dead life, poore mortall living ghost,
Woe's Scene, World's shame, Grave's due by life usurpt,

Brief abstract and record of tedious dayes,
Rest thy unrest on England's lawfull earth,
Unlawfully made drunke with innocents' blood (IV, 4).

. . . . . .

Dr. Tillyard adds that ' Queen Margaret is thinking of
Richard's crimes and the vengeance he will incur, yet by
repeating a phrase in four successive lines she expresses
unconsciously the new and frightful unity that God is to
construct out of Richard's impartial wickedness '.

He says, elsewhere, that ' the play can never come into
its own till acted as a sequel to the other three plays ' (*i.e.*
Henry the Sixth, Parts, I, II, and III) ' and with the solemnity
that we associate with the Dionysia at Athens '.

There is a relationship between this scene and the first
scene of *The Two Noble Kinsmen* — (one which I believe to
be Shakespeare's) :

> (*Enter three Queens in black, with veils stained, and wearing
> imperial crowns. The First Queen falls at the feet of Theseus ;
> the Second at the feet of Hypollyta ; the Third before Emilia.*)

First Queen

We are three Queens, whose sovereigns fell before
The wrath of cruel Creon ; who endure
The beaks of ravens, talents of the kites,
And pecks of crows, in the foul fields of Thebes ;
He will not suffer us to burn their bones

. . . . . .

And of thy boundless goodness, take some note
That for our crowned heads we have no roof
Save this, which is the lion's and the bear's
And vault to everything.

. . . . . .

Second Queen

              Lend us a knee,
But touch the ground for us no longer time
Than a dove's motion, when the head's pluck'd off ;
Tell him, if he i' the blood-siz'd field lay swoln,
Showing the sun his teeth, grinning at the moon,
What you would do !

The movement of this passage and that from *Richard the Third* are, however, totally different.

.   .   .   .

The great ceremonial of Darkness in which the Queens and Princesses mourn for the Platagenet blood that has been spilt, for the guilt of the slayers — takes place in the presence of one who seemed to himself, like Milton's Satan,

> . . . all but less than he
> Whom Thunder hath made greater.

Coleridge said, ' Pride of intellect is the characteristic of Richard. With this went his pride in his high place and supremacy of evil.'

This great, unquiet spirit, wrenched by Nature from his true shape, and turned to evil, said :

> . . . I was borne so high,
> Our Ayerie buildeth in the Cedar's top,
> And dallies with the Winde and scornes the Sunne.

> QUEEN MARGARET
> And turnes the Sunne to shade ; alas ! alas !
> Witnesse my Sonne, now in the shade of death ;
> Whose bright out-shining beames thy cloudy wrath
> Hath in eternall Darknesse folded up (I, 3).

The shadow from that ' hell-govern'd arme ' (I, 2) blotted out the sun.

And when Richard says,

> . . . I, in this weak piping time of peace,
> Have no delight to passe away the time,
> Unlesse to spy my Shadow in the Sunne
> And descant on mine owne Deformity (I, 1) :

we see the giant shadow spreading.[1]

In Richard, all the sins of the Plantagenets were heaped, like the mountain of deformity upon his back. But it was the isolation which fell upon him because of that deformity, that made him what he was : he who was

[1] See IV, 'Some General Notes on the Tragedies'.

> . . . curtail'd of this faire Proportion,
> Cheated of Feature by dissembling Nature,
> Deform'd, unfinish'd, sent before my time
> Into this breathing world, scarce halfe made up,
> And that so lamely and unfashionable
> That dogges barke at me as I halt by them (I, 1);

What was left to him except to watch the growth of terror as his shadow grew?

At last, in the night before Bosworth, the shadows of those he had sent to death came to confront the shadow thrown by his withered and all-withering arm. Then, for the first and last time, he knew fear.

For with those shadows came the knowledge of the Hell in his own bosom —

> What doe I feare? my Selfe? There's none else by:

— came the knowledge that he cannot fly from the murderer that is himself, the revenger that is himself and has avenged his sins upon himself, through loving himself.

> Is there a Murtherer heere? No. Yes, I am:
> Then flye. What, from my selfe . . . ? (V, 3)

Yet, in spite of his

> . . . severall sinnes, all used in each degree,

that

> Thronge to the bar, crying all ' Guilty! Guilty! '

in the heat of battle, his horse killed, he enacted:

> . . . more wonders than a man,
> Daring an opposite to every danger:

And, as one fallen from heaven,

> '. . . Darken'd so, yet shon
> Above them all th' Arch Angel: but his face
> Deep scars of Thunder had entrencht, but under Browes
> Of dauntless courage.' [1]

[1] *Paradise Lost.*

XIX

SOME GENERAL NOTES ON THE COMEDIES

SHAKESPEARE's Comedies, roughly, are of three kinds. In the first kind

> The Sommer still doth tend upon my state ;

as the Queen of the Fairies said in *A Midsommer-Night's Dreame*. And this is true even in tales of winter, and when

> . . . hoary-headed frosts
> Fall in the fresh lap of the crimson Rose,
> (*A Midsommer-Night's Dreame*, II, 1)

'There's sap in it yet' — in the world and in the heart.

In the second kind, the strong force of life fights and overcomes a thin and meagre living death — as in *All's Well that Ends Well*.

In the third kind there is separation ending in reunion and in reconciliation, — in peace of heart.

Some of the Comedies, again, are like Beatrice, who ' dreamed of unhappinesse and waked her selfe with laughing' (*Much Ado about Nothing*, II, 1).

Even anger is of the nature of the rose :

> DON JUAN : I had rather be a canker in the hedge than
> a rose in his grace ;
> (*Much Ado about Nothing*, I, 3)

And through all the plays — comedies and tragedies — sound the songs — sometimes epitomising the meaning of the play, sometimes hiding a strange, haunting wisdom — or coming to us only as ' naked ear-delighting absolute Melody — Melody that is just Melody and nothing else ; that glides into the ear, one knows not why . . . that sounds sad when we are merry and merry when we are sad '.[1] ' A musical thought ', said Carlyle, ' is spoken by a mind that has penetrated into the inmost heart of the thing ; detected the inmost mystery of it, namely, *the melody* that lies hidden in it, the inward harmony of coherence which is its soul, whereby it exists.'

.   .   .   .   .   .

The wisdom in these Comedies is ' the divine understanding and knowledge, which shall blossom in the time of the lily '.[2] For wisdom it is — flowering sometimes from what would seem to be the dry earth — or coming to us on a sudden wind of spring that brings whispers of immortality.

[1] Richard Wagner, *Posthumous Works.*
[2] Jakob Boehme, *The Signature of All Things.*

XX

'TWELFTH NIGHT'

'YOUTH'S a stuffe will not endure', sings Feste, the wise Fool, in one of the songs of which I have spoken, and it is the keynote of the play.

CURIO

Will you goe hunt, my lord?

DUKE

What, Curio?

CURIO

The Hart.

DUKE

Why so I doe (I, 1),

'Youth's a stuffe will not endure' — and the wild-wood love, the sound of the horn and of hunter and hunted, will soon be gone from the thickets of the heart.

Olivia swears

By the Roses of the Spring (III, 1),

forgetting that they fade, and that before another spring breaks her love will have withered, and another love will have taken its place.

In this play, as in the earlier *Comedy of Errors*, and in several other plays of Shakespeare, there are beings who have been cast upon a sea-shore, as we are cast, haphazard, upon this life, with, always, the sense that there were strange adventures in the past.

VIOLA

What Country, Friends, is this?

CAPTAIN

This is Illyria, Lady.

VIOLA

And what should I doe in Illyria ?
My brother he is in Elysium.
Perchance he is not drown'd : What think you, saylors ?
(I, 2)

Here is the beginning of the ineffable sea music which is at its most miraculous in *The Tempest*.

XXI

'*AS YOU LIKE IT*'

HAZLITT said of Shakespeare's Comedy that it is ' of the
pastoral or poetical cast. Folly is indigenous to the soil,
and shoots out with native, happy, unchecked luxuriance.
Inexhaustible invention reigns.'

In *As You Like It* the laughter is that of happiness, not
mirth. The spirit manifesting itself in the young people is
' like the gem of a vine, or the bud of a rose . . . the
principles of grace and sweetness ; they had the infancy of
knowledge, in which they read with the eye of a bird, and
speak with the tongue of a bee, and understand with the
heart of a child '.[1]

All thought is sweet-voiced and quick as the singing-
birds.

Rosalind, saying

Certainlie, a woman's thought runnes before her actions,

and Orlando, replying :

So do all thoughts ; they are winged (IV, 1),

speak the truth.

In the song ' Under the Greene-wood tree ' lies the
epitome, the core, of the play, as it is almost an impertinence
to point out.

Under the Greene-wood tree
Who loves to lye with me,
And turne his merry Note
Unto the sweet Bird's throte,
Come hither, come hither, come hither :
Heere shall he see
No enemy
But Winter and rough Weather.

.   .   .   .

[1] Jeremy Taylor, Sermon XXXI.

179

> Who doth ambition shunne
> And loves to live i' the Sunne,
> Seeking the food he eates
> And pleas'd with what he gets,
> Come hither, come hither, come hither :
> Heere shall he see
> No enemy
> But Winter and rough Weather (II, 4).

Here the line

> Come hither, come hither, come hither

has the actual sound of a wild bird-song. Do we not hear this very music falling from the boughs, each spring ?

On two of the other beings of this innocent world, Duke Frederick and Oliver, the elder brother of Orlando, — on these alone falls the shadow of the world. The Duke Senior has something of the sweet earthy heart of his own great creator. Like Shakespeare, like the first men to come into the world, he has ' eaten of the earth, and found it sweet '. All winter-hardness has gone from him, and from his follower, Jacques. The latter pities the poor stag,

> Left and abandon'd of his velvet friends ;

— the poor wounded creature whose

> big round teares
> Cours'd one another downe his innocent nose
> In pitteous chase ;

— he stands

> . . . weeping and commenting
> Upon the sobbing Deere

— seeing it deserted.

> Thus most invectively, he pierceth through
> The body of the Country, City, Court,
> Yea, and of this our life ; swearing that we
> Are meere usurpers, tyrants, and what's worse,
> To fright the Animals and to kill them up
> In their assign'd and native dwelling-place (II, 1).

The poor harmless beasts must not be invaded and injured. Mercy must reign.

Even on sin must one have pity :

DUKE SENIOR

Most mischeevous foule sin, in chiding sin :
For thou thy self has been a Libertine,
As sensuall as the brutish sting it self (II, 7) ;

Here, in this Paradise where man has regained his first innocence, the cold heart of the world is forgotten. Here

. . . feel we but the penalty of Adam,
The season's difference (II, 1) ;

But there are two nations, the young and the old. Poor Age sees itself for a moment through the eyes of youth, when Silvanus says to the old shepherd, Corin :

O Corin, that thou knewest how I doe love her !

CORIN

I partly guess, for I have lov'd ere now.

SILVANUS

No, Corin ; being old, thou canst not guesse,
Though in thy youth thou wast as true a lover
As ever sigh'd upon a midnight pillow (II, 4) ;

Time, and the hardness of men's hearts — these are the only enemies. The second of these has been left behind in the world ; there is still the first, but it is measured only by the lover's sighs.

ROSALIND : I pray you, what is't o'clocke ?

ORLANDO : You should aske me, what time o' day ; there's no clocke in the Forrest.

ROSALIND : Then there is no true lover in the Forrest ; else sighing every minute and groaning every hour would detect the lazie foote of Time as well as a clock (III, 2).

As for melancholy, Jacques says with truth :

I do love it better than laughing (IV, 1).

N

And it is, indeed, no darker, it glitters often like the dew upon the leaves.

One tragic and freezing darkness falls over the play, in the song ' Blow, blow, thou winter wind '.

But this, and the occasional grave shade cast by the older and more experienced beings — the Duke Senior and Jacques, these restful shadows, like forest boughs, are the only darknesses, and they do not fall upon the minds of the young.

Only one small shadow is cast by the world in the path of youth.

> O, how full of briers is this working-day world !

says one young girl to the other. And Celia replies :

> They are but burs, Cosen, throwne upon thee in holiday foolery : if we walke not in the trodden paths, our very petycoats will catch them.

To which Rosalind answers :

> I could shake them off my coat : these burs are in my heart (I, 3).

But we know that the burrs in the heart will soon fall away, and that the only darkness will be the shade Rosalind seeks :

> Ile tell thee, Aliena, I cannot be out of the sight of Orlando : Ill goe find a shaddow and sigh till he come.

> CELIA
> And Ile sleepe (IV, 1).

Do men die for love ?

> ' Leander, he would have lived many a fair yeare, though Hero had turned Nun, if it had not beene for a hot Midsomer Night; for, good youth, hee went but forth to wash himself in the Hellespont, and being taken with the crampe was drown'd ; and the foolish coroners of that age found it was Hero of Sestos. But these are all lies ; men have dyed from time to time, and worms have eaten them, but not for love.'

XXII

NOTE ON 'ALL'S WELL THAT ENDS WELL'

THE second kind of Comedy, as I said in the General Notes on the Comedies, is one in which the strong force of life fights against a thin and meagre living death. In *All's Well that Ends Well*, Helena, a strong, bright, rank flower, forces her powerful roots, her living strength, her passion for life, through the bleak air by which she is surrounded, towards her sun, Bertram.

' It is from my influence', said Folly in Erasmus' *Panegyrick upon Folly*, ' that the whole world receives her ferment of mirth and Jollity. . . .' Ferment, the saps and juices of the earth disturbed by Spring. But in this play even the Clown is thin and white like Winter, but with none of the sparkling bright quality of Jack Frost.

As Mr. van Doren has pointed out, he is ' as bleak and bitter as the air that blows through his old mistress's rooms. . . . Not only has she ' (the old Countess) ' hung her house with black in sign of her unfortunate widowhood ; she oppresses it with her thin, cold way of speaking, which is like that of Lafeu, the old lord who haunts it with her, and who is as far from being a Polonius or a Menenius as the peeled stick is from a budded stem.'

Lafeu is an aged bore, pleased with his withered platitudes : ' 'Twas a good lady, 'twas a good lady. We may pick a thousand salads ere we light on such another herb — ' he says of Helena.

And we see again the plant ruled by a sun, amid the general withering.

No wonder that, in such an air, Helena, loving the braggart Parolles for Bertram's sake, feels a liking for him, too, because of his strong growth, his will to live :

And yet I know him a notorious Liar,
Thinke him a great way foole, solie a coward ;
Yet these fixed evils sit so fit in him,
That they take place, when Vertue's steely bones
Looke bleake in the cold wind : withall, full oft we see
Cold wisedom waiting on superfluous follie (I, 1).

And here again, in the case of Parolles, we see a character
pardoned for his faults, because of his force of life. Shewn,
at last, as what he is, he declares

> Simply the thing I am
> Shall make me live (IV, 3),

and, with this, attains a kind of grandeur.
But Helena's strength of life is greater still :

I am undone : There is no living, none,
If Bertram be away. It were all one
That I should love a bright particular starre
And thinke to wed it, he is so above me :
In his bright radience and collaterall light
Must I be comforted, not in his sphere (I, 1).

' Everything ', said Thomas Vaughan, ' hath its character
pressed upon it by its Star for some peculiar effect, especially
by the Star which doth principally govern it : And these
characters contain, and retain in them the peculiar natures,
virtues, and roots of their Stars, and produce the like operations upon other things, on which they are reflected.' [1]

He says, elsewhere (*Lumen de Lumine*), ' There is not
an Herb here below, but he hath a *star* in *Heaven above*, and
the star strikes him with her *Beames* and sayes to him
" *grow* " '.

' The bright particular star ', says Mr. van Doren, ' is
not the only strong thing here. Helena speaks often of
stars, and the fact that she does, symbolizes her solitary
blazing brightness in the play. . . . One of her favourite
words is " Nature ", and there is much of it in her. She

---

[1] *Magica Adamica.*

has body as well as mind. . . . There is nothing frail about
Helena, whose passion is secret and unmeasured : and because her body is real her mind is gifted with a rank, a
sometimes masculine fertility.'

Helena *is* like Nature ruled by a planet.

' Virginity ', says Parolles, ' murthers it selfe, and should
be buried in highwayes, out of all sanctified limit, as a
desperate Offendresse against nature.'

Helena sighs :

> That Wishing well had not a body in't,
> Which might be felt ; that we, the poorer borne,
> Whose baser starres do shut us up in wishes,
> Might with effects of them follow our friends,
> And show what we alone must thinke, which never
> Returnes us thanks [1] (I, 1).

She is irresistible with the force of Spring, the ferment, the
mounting sap :

> Our remedies oft in ourselves do lie
> Which we ascribe to heaven : the fated skye
> Gives us free scope : onely doth backward pull
> Our slow designes when we our selves are dull.
> What power is it which mounts my love so hye ;
> That makes me see, and cannot feede mine eye ?
> The mightiest space in fortune Nature brings
> To joyne like likes, and kisse like native things (I, 1).

[1] ' And show by realities what we now must only think.'—JOHNSON.

XXIII

SOME NOTES ON THE TEXTURE
OF ' A MIDSUMMER-NIGHT'S DREAM '

' THE thing is a piece of profound verdure ', said Keats, in his annotations to the play.

And excepting for the great passage that begins with the words

> The course of true love never did runne smoothe

(and of this I shall speak in a moment), there is no darkness excepting that of the summer night, and the shadows cast on the moonlight by that ' profound verdure '.

Although there is a word spoken about the great Duke returning from Thebes as a conqueror, the sound of war and turmoil is far away. There is no memory of Theseus' adventures in the Labyrinth — and of the monster who was begot by a bull and had the blood of the Sun in his veins — (for was not the bellowing Pasiphae daughter of the Sun ?) — instead of the bull-headed monster of infinite menace, infinite evil, there is the innocent country bumpkin Bottome, with his ass-head crowned with flowers.

Only the Fairies remember the seduction of Ariadne,[1] sister and priestess of the Minotaur — Princess, or Bee-goddess.

It is true that, at the beginning, old age tries to cast a frost on the lives of the young lovers, and, in the midst of the youthful warmth, the eternal moonlight of the Mid-summer Night, in which the lovers, like the fairies, are

> Following darknesse like a dreame,

come these lines, whose richness and dark splendour might

---

[1] For these references to Ariadne, see Marguerite Yourcenar's *Mythologie*, Lettres Françaises.

have grown (as far as the movement, the slow magnificence, are concerned) in the play *Antony and Cleopatra*, — although the lovers of *A Midsummer-Night's Dream* are younger than Antony and his Queen : it is a youthful passion that speaks here, and not luxury ; so it is nearer in blood to the last scenes of *Romeo and Juliet.*

LYSANDER

The course of true love never did runne smoothe ;
But, either it was different in bloud,—

HERMIA

O crosse ! too high to be enthrall'd to lowe.[1]

LYSANDER

Or else misgraffed, in respect of yeares,—

HERMIA

O spight ! Too olde to be ingag'd to yong.

LYSANDER

Or else it stood upon the choice of friends,—

HERMIA

O hell ! to choose love by another's eie.[2]

LYSANDER

Or, if there were a sympathie in choise,
Warre, death, or sicknesse did lay siege to it,
Making it momentarie as a sound,
Swift as a shadowe, short as any dreame,
Briefe as the lightning in the collied night,
That, in a spleene, unfolds both heaven and earth,
And ere a man hath power to say ' Beholde ! '
The jawes of darknesse do devoure it up :
So quicke bright things come to confusion (I, 1).

So much for the grandeur of the summer darkness.   But

. . . thoughts and dreames and sighes,
Wishes and teares . . .

are but

. . . poor Fancie's followers (I, 1),

---

[1] Theobald changed ' love ' to ' low '.   [2] ' eyes ', Quarto.

says Hermia, and they are as quickly gone.

The miraculous shape of this splendour of the longer passage quoted above is due to the particular placing of the alliterative *s*'s — each word containing an *s* sound having its own particular shape, height, or depth, its own degree of sharpness — (this last effect being given by an attached *h*) — its own peculiar length or shortness, softness or body. These variations have much effect upon the rhythm. The first syllables of ' sympathie ' and ' sicknesse ', for instance, although the *y* and the *i* are assonances, are not equal in length. ' Sympathie ' has a moderately long, stretching first syllable, and it remains on a level, whereas the first syllable of ' sicknesse ' is (though very slightly) shorter ; it is also rounded by the *ck*. There is a drop from ' siege ' to ' sound '. ' Sound ' is longer than ' Swift ' and has a different shape — it stretches into space and then dies away again, whilst ' Swift ', though short, has the faintest possible movement, *within* its one syllable, owing to the *f*, which is, however, stopped, as soon as heard, by the *t*. ' Spleene ', again, is so long a word, owing to the stretching *e*'s, that although, actually, it has but one syllable, it almost equals, in length, a word of two syllables.

The shape is largely the result, too, of the alliterative *d*'s of ' darknesse ' and ' devoure ' — alliterations that gather the rhythm together. But, above all, the movement of this wonderful passage is given by the changing vowel-lengths, brightening and lengthening, dimming and shrinking, and by the particular place in which the assonances and dissonances are put, — the change from the youthful warmth of those assonances ' bloud ' and ' love ', to the heightening despair of the dissonances of ' choose ', ' eie '.

Then there is the darkening of the sound from ' spleene ' to ' man ' (these dissonances being placed in exactly the same position in the line), the brilliant sharpness of ' quicke ', ' bright ', then the dulling-down to the thickness of ' come ' and the dusty shapelessness of ' confusion ' — the drop into darkness, into chaos, of those last words :

> come to confusion.

Never has there been a more magical use of sound to convey meaning than in this play. Let us consider various passages.

Long stretches of moonlight are given by the vowels (as used in their particular places in the lines) of this phrase from Theseus' opening speech :

> O ! me thinkes how slow
> This old Moone wanes ;

first, internal assonances, then a wonderful fading dissonance (Moone wanes) ; and with that, we move from the moonlight into shadow.

Echo after echo of splendours and of dream.

A little later, there is the beauty given by the echo (almost at opposite ends of lines divided from each other) of a rhyme.

> But earthlier happie is the Rose distill'd,
> Than that which withering on the virgin thorne
> Growes, lives, and dies, in single blessedness ! (I, 1)

Later, in the same scene, — in

> To-morrow night, when Phoebe doth behold
> Her silver visage in the watery glasse,
> Decking with liquid pearle the bladed grass,

the pause is so long after ' pearle ' it seems like a long stretch of moonlight.

To my belief, the first Fairy Song is printed wrongly in certain modern editions.

To print it thus :

> Over hil, over dale,
> Thorough bush, thorough briar,
> Over parke, over pale,
> Thorough flood, thorough fire

seems to me wrong, because the pause at the end of each

line makes the fairy move slowly.   Whereas, if it is printed thus :

> Over hil, over dale, thorough bush, thorough briar,
> Over parke, over pale, thorough flood, thorough fire —

the pause owing to the long vowels is less like a hesitation than like the stretching of wings.   The fairy was in a hurry.[1]
Let us take this incredible beauty from the beginning :

> Over hil, over dale, thorough bush, thorough briar,
> Over parke, over pale, thorough flood, thorough fire,
> I do wander everie where, swifter than the Moon's sphere ;
> And I serve the Fairy Queene, to dew her orbs upon the
>   green :
> The Cowslips tall her pensioners bee ;
> In their gold coats spots you see ;
> Those be Rubies, Fairie favors,
> In those freckles live their savors :
> I must go seeke some dew-drops heere,
> And hang a pearle in every cowslip's eare (II, 1).

In the line

> The Cowslips tall her pensioners bee ;

the three-syllabled word ' pensioners ' has a little trembling sound, like that of dew being shaken from a flower.

Note, too, the effect on the rhythm of the rising, brightening dissonances and the darkening dissonances, and, too, of the alliterations in the first two lines, — the effect is brought about, also, by the internal rhymes ' dale ' and ' pale ' put at exactly that place within the lines : ' hil ' brightens into ' dale ', ' bush ' deepens into ' briar ', then darkens into ' parke '.   This rises again and brightens into ' pale ' — so that we see the fairy flying through the sunlight and shadow of the day that deepened into the night of this immortal summer.

[1] ' . . . *thorough* bush, *thorough* briar,
      . . . *thorough* flood, *thorough* fire '
— so it is printed in the First Quarto.   But in the First Folio it is printed ' Through ', which must surely be wrong.

Again, in the line

> In their gold coats spots you see;

— after the bright assonances of 'gold coats' we have a slightly darker dissonance to 'coats' in 'spots'.

A fresh and lovely balance is given to the lines

> Those be Rubies, Fairie favors,
> In those freckles live their savors :

by the fact that though 'Rubies' and 'freckles' appear to be equivalent in length, actually they are not so. 'Rubies' is longer, because of the vowel-sound.

But the whole scene is a miracle.

An enchanted beauty is given by the lingering *l*'s in 'Lady' and 'Land' of Titania's

> Then I must be thy Lady ; but I know
> When thou hast stolne away from Fairy Land,

— a sound echoed again in 'love' and 'Phillida', of the succeeding lines :

> And in the shape of Corin sate all day,
> Playing on pipes of Corne, and versing love
> To amorous Phillida.

There is a strange darkening and concentration, changing of shape, from 'Corin' to the sound of 'Corne'.

After these lines, the beauty of sound is brought about by the perpetual darkening and brightening of the vowel-sounds, the echoes of brightness and of darkness, and by the strange effect of the internal and external dissonantal *o*'s.

> Didst thou not lead him through the glimmering night
> From Perigouna, whom he ravished ?
> And make him with faire Ægle breake his faith,
> With Ariadne, and Antiopa ?

The dimmed *i*'s fall often upon unstressed syllables. The *a*'s, after the long brightness of the 3rd line, are dimmed

in the 4th, bring about, as they die away on the word
' Antiopa ' (with its momentary brightening *i*), a transcend-
ental beauty.

Later, there is a marvel of air-thin texture, woven upon
the loom of the moonlight and shadow :

> The Fairy land buyes not the childe of me.
> His mother was a votaresse of my Order ;
> And, in the spiced Indian aire, by night,
> Full often hath she gossipt by my side,
> And sat with me on Neptune's yellow sands,
> Marking the embarked traders on the flood ;
> When we have laught to see the sailes conceive
> And grow big-bellied with the wanton winde ;
> Which she, with pretty and with swimming gait
> Following, — (her wombe then rich with my yong
>   squire,) —
> Would imitate, and saile upon the Land,
> To fetch me trifles, and returne againe,
> As from a voyage, rich with merchandize (II, 1).

But before this, and coming immediately after the passage
about Ariadne and Antiopa, there is a wonderful use of
falling dissonances, adding strangeness, and coming like a
faint breath of cooler air, gone in a moment, in this summer
night.

> The Ox hath therefore stretch'd his yoake in vaine,
> The Ploughman lost his sweat, and the greene corne
> Hath rotted ere his youth attain'd a beard :

After this, what miracles are performed by the use of
sharpening *r*'s, as in the first two lines of

> The seasons alter : hoary-headed frosts
> Fall in the fresh lap of the crimson Rose,
> And on old Hyem's thinne and icie crowne
> An odorous Chaplet of sweet sommer buds
> Is, as in mockery, set.

Here, the beauty of sound is due as much to the deep
breath of the alliterative *h*'s (' hoary-headed ') and the dim-

ming *f*'s which succeed these, as to the wonderful design of dissonantal *o*'s.

This beautiful use of the *r* schemes is noticeable again in Titania's speech to her attendant fairies — and in this case it has an effect like that of the faint roughness of certain leaves.

> Feede him with Apricockes and Dewberries,
> With purple Grapes, Green Figs, and Mulberries.
> The honie-bags steale from the humble-Bees,
> And for night-tapers crop their waxen thighes,
> And light them at the fierie Glow-wormes eyes,
> To have my love to bed, and to arise ;
> And pluck the wings from painted Butterflies
> To fan the moonbeams from his sleeping eies :
> Nod to him, Elves, and do him curtesies (III, 1).

Here, there is a wonderful movement, as if faint moon-light and dew were being woven into a texture on a shuttle of the summer airs. The change from ' *honie*-bags ' to ' *humble*-Bees ' in line 3 gives a faint velvetiness to the texture, like the coat of the bees. In the last line, all has become dim, with the smaller *e*'s.

Here, as elsewhere, it is evident that Shakespeare did not ' omit the enquiry how Butterflies and breezes move their four wings ', and that he has made full use of the results of that enquiry.

Such is the ' sommer's distillation ', until the moment when the practical fairies begin their sweet work :

> And we Fairies, that do runne
>   By the triple Hecate's teame,
> From the presence of the Sunne,
>   Following darknesse like a dreame,
> Now are frollicke ; not a Mouse
> Shall disturbe this hallowed house :
> I am sent with broome before,
> To sweep the dust behinde the doore.

— the dust of the day, the dust of mortality.

XXIV

TWO NOTES ON 'THE MERCHANT OF VENICE'

I

THIS seems to this reader like two plays, loosely bound together.

What is the connecting link? A golden wall of beautiful, healthful, laughing beings against which an image of disaster creeps?

Dowden says, 'The Merchant himself . . . is a central point at which may meet the contending forces of hatred and charity embodied in the persons of Shylock and the Lady of Belmont'.

. . . 'Charity?' . . . Perhaps.

When Bassanio says to her

> We should hold day with the Antipodes,
> If you would walke in absence of the Sunne (V, 1),

he is not, I think, speaking only of her golden beauty, but of the quality she represents.

But one foreshadowing of the true meaning of the play lies in Morocco's

> Mislike me not for my complexion,
> The shadow'd livery of the burnish'd sun,
> To whom I am a neighbour and near bred (II, 1).

The golden beauty, the prosperity of Venice, cannot speak to Shylock without pouring insults on his race.

But the epitome of the play lies in two sentences, — in Shylock's

> The villainy you teach me I will execute, and it shall go hard but I will better the instruction (III, 1).

194

And in these appalling lines, spoken by Gratiano to Shylock :

> Thou almost mak'st me waver in my faith
> To hold opinion with Pythagoras,
> That soules of animals infuse themselves
> Into the trunkes of men ; thy currish spirit
> Govern'd a Wolfe, who, hang'd for humane slaughter,
> Even from the Gallowes did his fell soule fleet,
> And whilst thou layest in thy unhallow'd dam,
> Infus'd it selfe in thee : for thy desires
> Are wolfish, bloody, starv'd, and ravenous (IV, 1).

That great and terrible speech, condemning, *apparently*, the criminal, — actually exculpates him, and places the guilt, the condemnation, on the ' miserable, mad, mistaking eyes ' of mankind.

In the dark centuries, blind punishments were wreaked by mankind upon poor beasts who sinned because they had only their instincts to guide them — or who were sinless but had been used for sport by Nature.

Such punishments were meted out to a sow who, convicted in France in 1457 of ' murder flagrantly committed on the person of Johann Martin, aged five ', was sentenced to be hanged by the hind feet from a tree or gibbet, and so died in unutterable torture. Her six sucklings were reprieved, since there was no evidence against them. Another sow, convicted of the murder of a human being, was hanged *wearing white gloves* — (the horror of the mind of the being who devised such a touch — it comes straight from hell !).
. . . A cow was sentenced to be shot and placed in an uncovered grave for killing a woman near Leipsic. A poor cock was burned alive as a sorcerer, because by some cruel process of Nature his sex changed to that of a hen, and he laid an egg.

Thus darkness was punished, by a darkness which came into men's minds from Hell. Is it likely that such punishments should go unpunished ? Are not our criminals those that our civilisation has brought down upon us ?

Shakespeare saw, with the eyes of the spirit, what Lombroso, Havelock Ellis, and other scientists were to see, centuries after, with the eyes of the body.

' " Society prepares crimes," as Quetelet said ; " the criminal is the instrument that executes them." " The social environment ", Lacassagne has well said, " is the cultivation medium of criminality ; the criminal is the microbe, an element which only becomes important when it finds the medium which causes it to ferment : every society has the criminals that it deserves." '—HAVELOCK ELLIS, *The Criminal.*

'I was deputed to make the post-mortem' (on a murderer), ' and on laying open the skull I found on the occipital part, exactly on the spot where a spine is found in the normal skull, a distinct depression which I named median occipital fossa, because of its situation precisely in the middle of the occiput as in inferior animals, especially rodents. This depression, as in the case of animals, was correlated with the hypertrophy of the vermis, known in birds as the middle cerebellum.

' This was not merely an idea, but a revelation. At the sight of that skull, I seemed to see, all of a sudden, lighted up as a vast plain under a flaming sky, the problem of the nature of the criminal. . . .'—CESARE LOMBROSO, Introduction to his daughter Gina Lombroso Ferrero's *Criminal Man According to the Classification of Cesare Lombroso).*

II

Notes on the Versification of a Passage in Act V, Scene I

If we take the first six lines :

The moone shines bright : in such a night as this,
When the sweet winde did gently kisse the trees

> And they did make no noyse, in such a night
> Troylus me thinkes mounted the Troian walls,
> And sigh'd his soule toward the Grecian tents,
> Where Cressid lay that night.

we shall find that the calm moonlit beauty of the sound is
due to the rising dissonances of 'kisse' and 'trees' in the
2nd line, and their darker dissonance 'noyse' in the 3rd, —
and also to the difference in the wave-lengths of their vowels,
those of 'trees' and 'noyse' being longer than that of
'kisse'. 'Troylus' in the 4th line is a kind of broken echo
of 'noyse' — is, as it were, a dark broken shadow; while
'lay' in the 6th line gives balance to the rhythm by being
a softer echo of 'make' in the 3rd, placed in exactly the
same position in the line.

In the next eight lines:

> . . . In such a night
> Did Thisbe fearefully o'ertrip the dewe,
> And saw the Lyon's shadow ere himselfe,
> And ranne dismay'd away.
> In such a night
> Stood Dido with a willow in her hand
> Upon the wilde sea bankes, and waft her Love
> To come againe to Carthage.

great beauty is given by the softening, drooping echo of
'Dido', 'willow' (an example of Shakespeare's genius in
the use of the falling foot), by the alliteration of 'willow',
'wilde', and 'waft' (this is one of those rare examples
where alliteration does not give a strong emphasis) — and
by the fact that in the 4th line, the word 'dismay'd', and
in the 8th line, the word 'againe', echo the 'lay' of

> Where Cressid lay that night.

When we come to:

> In such a night
> Medea gathered the inchanted hearbs
> That did renew old Eson.

O

> In such a night
> Did Jessica steale from the wealthy Jewe,
> And with an Unthrift Love did runne from Venice,
> As far as Belmont.

we shall see that 'Medea' is a broken (and softening, falling) echo of 'sea'; and 'Eson' is a shrunken echo of 'Medea'. 'Jewe', again, is an echo of 'renew', and all this gives balance, affects the movement of the lines.

XXV

TWO EARLY COMEDIES

I

'*LOVE'S LABOUR'S LOST*'

THE ordinary conversations of this play are glancing and light as a bird's feathers — the wit changes and narrows suddenly into rhymes that are sharp as a bird's song — rhymes catching at and holding the light, sharp and quick as the eyes of a bird.

In the Third Scene of the Fourth Act, the King utters words whose sense (but not whose sound — that is not yet the utterance of the god) stretches and sweeps into infinity :

> O me ! with what strict patience have I sat,
> To see a King transformed to a Gnat ;
> To see great Hercules whipping a Gigge,
> And profound Solomon to tune a Jygge,
> And Nestor play at push-pin with the boyes,
> And Critticke Tymon laugh at idle toyes !

A beginning only.

Yet in this play we have this real magnificence, in the midst of laughter :

ARMADO : The sweet War-man is dead and rotten ; sweet chuckes, beat not the bones of the buried ; when he breathed, he was a man (V, 2).

Sometimes there is a strange, clownish moon-struck beauty, as in the Second Scene of the Fourth Act, where it is achieved by bringing together two far-off likenesses :

> DULL
> You two are book-men : Can you tell me by your wit,
> What was a month old at Cain's birth, that's not five weeks
> old as yet ?

HOLOFERNES

Dictynna, Goodman Dull; Dictynna, Goodman Dull.

DULL

What is Dictynna?

NATHANIEL

A title to Phoebe, to Luna, to the Moone.

HOLOFERNES

The Moone was a month old when Adam was no more;
And raught not to five weekes when he came to five-score.
The allusion holds in the exchange.

DULL: 'Tis true indeed: the Collusion holds in the exchange.
HOLOFERNES: God comfort thy capacity! I say, the allusion
holds in the exchange.
DULL: And I say that the pollusion holds in the exchange, For
the Moone is never but a month old; and I say beside that
'twas a Pricket that the Princess kill'd.

The connection in these moonshine minds? That between
the horns of the young moon and of the young deer.
Before this, Holofernes had said:

The Deare was, as you know, sanguis, in blood; ripe as
a Pomewater, who now hangeth like a jewell in the eare of
Caelo, the sky, the welken, the heaven; and anon falleth
like a crab on the face of Terra, the soyle, the land, the earth.

Always there is this strange flight of sense into Folly's
heaven, — then comes a fall from that heaven — down and
down, on to Terra, the soyle, the land, the earth.

. . . . . .

Often we find, in the Princess's own words . . . 'wit
turned fool: folly in wisdom hatch'd', and sometimes in
this, as in the other Comedies, the sense, the wit, this flight
into Folly's heaven will borrow the body of a pun.

In this play, Costard, being given a 'remuneration',
says (III, 1),

Remuneration! O! that's the Latin word for three farthings.

Then, to Berowne :

> Pray you, sir, how much carnation ribbon may a man
> buy for a remuneration ?
> BEROWNE : What is a remuneration ?
> COSTARD : Marry, sir, half-penny farthing.
> BEROWNE : Why, then, three-farthings' worth of silk.
>
> .   .   .   .   .   .
>
> (*Gives him a shilling.*) There's thy guerdon : go.
> COSTARD : Gardon. O sweet Gardon ! better than remunera-
> tion ; a 'leven-pence farthing better. Most sweet Gardon !

And one sees his fortune growing like flowers (carnations,
perhaps, the colour of the longed-for ribbon), out of the
original narrow earth of the three farthings.

II

'*THE COMEDY OF ERRORS*'

Even in this play (one of the earliest), there is the
grandeur, the fullness of life of the great creator — as in
these lines of Adriana's :

> For know, my love, as easie mayst thou fall
> A drop of water in the breaking gulfe,
> And take unmingled thence that drop againe,
> Without addition or diminishing,
> As take from me thyselfe and not me too (II, 2).

(Of this, Saintsbury says : ' the transport and the trans-
mutation lie . . . most in the management of the metre,
the alternative check and rush of the now sundered, now
overlapping lines — the perfection of the entire phrase,
prosodic and poetic '.)

Antipholus of Syracuse says to his slave, the fool
Dromio of Syracuse :

When the Sunne shines let foolish gnats make sport,
But creepe in crannies when he hides his beames (II, 2).

We know from whose hand came those lines :

'Something of the lightness and brightness of his sunny
and fiery spirit gives light to all.' [1]

[1] This was said by Swinburne of a work by Nash — but it applies strongly to
The Comedy of Errors.

XXVI

THE LATER PLAYS

' AFTER the darkness of the Tragedies, which, however, as
it has been said, brought out the stars, there is here a
beautiful and serene illumination. Expressed in a way
suitable to drama, there seems to be a recognition of some
divine influence presiding over human life. The joy at the
close of each play has in it something more sacred than
the gladness and mirth of the earlier Comedies. . . . The
bonds of love are broken only to be reunited in a higher
place . . . the incident of a lost child or lost children
restored to their parents is repeated in each play ; Cymbeline
recovers the sons who in their infancy had been stolen from
him ; Pericles recovers Marina ; Hermione once more
embraces Perdita ; Alonzo rejoices at the sight of Ferdinand
whom it was supposed the sea had engulfed.'—EDMUND
DOWDEN, *Introduction to Cymbeline* (The Oxford Shakespeare).

XXVII

SOME NOTES ON 'THE WINTER'S TALE'

I

The Fertility Symbols

THE reason for the name is obvious. The little Mamillius said 'a sad tale's best for winter'. — But it was a child who was speaking, to whom time is long. He could not foresee the spring.

Apollo, as Dr. Tillyard has pointed out, is the dominant god in *The Winter's Tale* — the Sun, that brings all to life, — the symbol of fertility.

The Clown sees gold scattered upon the ground :

> Gold ! all gold !

and the old Shepherd replies :

> This is Faiery Gold, boy, and 'twill prove so (III, 3) ;

And we see the gold of the spring and early summer sprouting among the grass.

Gold is not hard and cold, — but seems a property of, and part of, the Sun.

Autolycus, like a thieving sweet wind, running on feet as quick as this, says to the Clown whom he has robbed :

> Your purse is not hot enough to purchase your spice (IV, 2).

To Perdita, who is another Persephone, there is, however, no winter darkness, no winter spite. But Age and its snows have sweetness remembered from summer :

> . . . Reverend Sirs,
> For you there's Rosemary and Rue ; These keepe
> Seeming and savour all the Winter long.

All are welcome — all seasons are loved and enriched by the life-giving Sun.

> . . . Here's flowres for you :
> Hot Lavender, Mints, Savory, Marioram,
> The Mary-gold, that goes to bed wi' the Sun,
> And with him rises weeping : these are flowres
> Of middle summer, and I thinke they are given
> To men of middle age.   You are very welcome (IV, 3).

The creative processes of Nature, healing and re-making all, overcoming the winter death, — these rule the play. At the thought of violation of faith :

> Let Nature crush the sides o' the earth together
> And marre the seeds within !

says Florizel (IV, 3).

All goodness is as the rising of the sap ; and, hearing of Camillo's proposed plan, Florizel says :

> There is some sappe in this.

Leontes tells Florizel and Perdita that they are

> Welcome hither,
> As is the Spring to the Earth (V, 1).

That warmth of spring comes again to the lips of the Queen that had seemed cold and still as winter.   Neither winter nor the seeming state of death are eternal.   Proserpine returns to the loving and waiting arms.

II

Notes on the Use of Elisions in Act IV, Scene 3

As I have pointed out elsewhere, elisions in blank verse are often but *pretended* elisions, and are an excuse for variety, since the supposedly elided syllables exist and are not muted. Sometimes, as in *King Lear*, these pretended elisions produce

the effect of the shaking of a huge and smoky volcano —
(we find this effect, too, though it is less vast, over and over
again in *Paradise Lost*) — or they swell the line, moving it
slightly forward, rearing it upward, like the beginning of
a tidal wave, and presaging the final break and the shattering
roar of that wave.   In Perdita's speech, in Act IV, Scene 3,
of *The Winter's Tale*, pretended elisions give a line the faintest
possible increased length, or produce a faint dip in the line
(the word 'Flowers', for instance, has this last-mentioned
effect) :

> . . . O Proserpina !
> For the Flowers now that frighted thou let'st fall
> From Dysses' Waggon ! Daffodils,
> That come before the Swallow dares, and take
> The windes of March with beauty ; Violets dim,
> But sweeter than the lids of Juno's eyes
> Or Cytherea's breath ; pale Prime-roses,
> That dye unmarried, ere they can behold
> Bright Phoebus in his strength (a Malady
> Most incident to Maids) ; bold Oxlips and
> The Crowne Imperiall ; Lillies of all kinds,
> (The flowre-de-Luce being one).   O ! these I lacke
> To make you Garlands of, and my sweet friend,
> To strew him o'er and o'er.

If we examine this, we shall find that the beauty of the sound
owes much to the fluctuations caused by the pretendedly
elided syllables in ' Flowres ' and ' Violets ', and to Shakespeare's genius in the use of the falling foot — ('Proserpina',
' Cytherea ' — names which fall with a flower-like softness
and sweetness).   Then, again, much beauty is given to the
fact that the last syllable of ' Daffodils ' echoes the vowel-
sound of ' Dysses ' and that ' lids ' is an echo (but the
faintest possible fraction higher) of ' dim '.   Note the change
in the texture when we come to

> . . . pale Prime-roses,
> That dye unmarried, ere they can behold
> Bright Phoebus in his strength.

Here all is brighter, owing to the high echoing *i* sounds following the dim *i* of 'lids'. Nor is this the result of association only, for in the rest of the fragment the texture varies, growing richer with the sound of 'bold' and 'Crowne' in the phrase

> . . . bold Oxlips and
> The Crowne Imperiall;

One of the most wonderful of all examples of Shakespeare's genius in the use of the falling foot is in Desdemona's line:

> Sing all a greene willough must be my Garland.

I was once privileged to hear this miraculous line changed (in a song) to

> Sing all a greene willough my Garland must be ! ! !

XXVIII
'*PERICLES*'

PERICLES, PRINCE OF TYRE was entered in the Stationers' *Register* May 20, 1608.

Steevens believes it to be the work of a friend 'whose interest . . . Shakespeare was anxious to promote. He therefore improved the dialogue in many cases.'

I would have believed, rather, that it was an early play by Shakespeare, put aside, and then taken up again and retouched. But Dowden says this is impossible. And yet it contains two supreme grandeurs, — one, almost at the end of the play, epitomises the meaning — the theme, as well as Marina's beauty :

> . . . Yet thou dost look
> Like Patience gazing on Kings' graves, and smiling
> Extremity out of act (V, 1).

which would seem to presage some of the wonders in the later works, although they are of an infinitely lesser greatness and command.

PERICLES
> Wind, rain, and thunder, remember, earthly man
> Is but a substance that must yield to you ;
> And I, as fits your nature, do obey you (II, 1) ;

is an example.

Did this come from the hand that wrote, the heart that felt, the soul that suffered the giant world-pangs felt by Lear ? It seems like a small reflection.

Again, are these lines a foreshadowing of the later world-shaking wonders ?

PERICLES
> . . . The blind mole casts
> Copp'd hills towards heaven, to tell the earth is throng'd
> With man's oppression ; and the poor worm doth die for't
> (I, 1).

Here, surely, is the very movement of Shakespeare —
superb, but not yet brought to its supreme magnificence.

In this earlier passage :

> You're a fair viol, and your sense the strings,
> Who, finger'd to make man his lawful music,
> Would draw heaven down and all the gods to hearken ;
> But being play'd upon before your time,
> Hell only danceth at so harsh a chime.
> Good sooth, I care not for you (I, 1),

the 4th and 5th lines have a strange singing music, but
they are, in a way, reminiscent of Tourneur, or of Middleton,
rather than of Shakespeare.

The play is infinitely puzzling. Could the author of
certain of the Sonnets have written these lines ? —

SIMONIDES
And she is fair, too, is she not ?

PERICLES
As a fair day in summer ; wondrous fair (II, 5).

I think not. Here is someone imitating the handwriting of
the god.

And did the hand that wrote (in, after all, a compara-
tively early play) the miracle beginning with the line

> Now the hungry Lyon rores,

write, also, these unhappy lines ? —

> Now sleep y-slaked hath the rout ;
> No din but snores the house about,
> Made louder by the o'erfed breast
> Of this most pompous marriage-feast.
> The Cat, with eyne of burning coale,
> Now circles fore the Mouse's hole ;
> And Crickets sing at the oven's mouth,
> E'er the blither for their drouth (III, 1).

It is unthinkable.

Yet, in the very scene to which this poverty-stricken,

ragged, thin, bloodless misery is attached as Prologue,
comes this passage :

> Thou God of this great vast, rebuke these surges,
> Which wash both heaven and hell ; and thou, that hast
> Upon the windes command, bind them in Brasse,
> Having call'd them from the deep. O ! still
> Thy deafening, dreadful thunders ; gently quench
> Thy nimble, sulphurous flashes. O ! how, Lychorida,
> How does my Queen ? Thou stormest venomously ;
> Wilt thou spit all thyself ? The Seaman's whistle
> Is as a whisper in the ears of death,
> Unheard.

A strange mixture, in which the 2nd and 3rd lines, and
the last line and a half, would seem to be Shakespeare's.
Then comes this greatness, which is unmistakable :

> A terrible Child-bed hast thou had, my Dear ;
> No light, no fire : the unfriendly Elements
> Forgot thee utterly ; nor have I time
> To give thee hallow'd to thy grave, but straight
> Must cast thee, scarcely Coffin'd, in the ooze ;
> Where, for a Monument upon thy bones,
> And aye-remaining lamps, the belching Whale
> And humming water must o'erwhelm thy Corps,
> Lying with simple shells !

We are safe in the hands of the god.—Yet this does not
seem like work of the early period — but more like that
wonder the end of *Timon of Athens* — though other passages
would seem, when they bear his stamp, to have been written
before he reached his maturity.

Swinburne says of this scene : ' As in his opening speech
. . . we heard all the clangour and resonance of warring
wind and sea, so now we hear a sound of sacred and spiritual
music as solemn as the central monochord of the inner
main itself '.

It is in majestic contrast to ' the flower-soft loveliness

of maiden lamentation over the flower-strewn seaside grave
of Marina's old sea-tossed nurse', to quote Swinburne
once more.

' Music ', said Wagner, in his book on Beethoven,
' would seem to reveal the most secret sense of scene, action,
environment.'

This is true, also, of poetry. The peculiar bright light
that we find near the sea, the sharpness and, one might
almost say, the unheard noise (that seems always to be
there, but never quite to reach our ears) — of the sea-airs
— these shine and blow in the lines to which Swinburne
referred :

> (*Enter Marina, with a Basket of Flowers*) :
> No, I will rob Tellus of her weed,
> To strew thy green with flowers ; the yellows, blues,
> The purple Violets, and Marigolds,
> Shall as a carpet hang upon thy grave,
> While summer dayes do last.   Aye me ! poor Maid,
> Born in a tempest, when my Mother di'd,
> This world to me is like a lasting storme,
> Whirring me from my friends (IV, 1).

XXIX

‘ *THE TEMPEST* ’

‘ With the general notion of order Shakespeare was always concerned, with man's position on the chain of being between beast and angel acutely during his tragic period ; but only in *The Tempest* does he seem to consider the chain itself ’ (*The Elizabethan World Picture*, E. M. W. Tillyard).[1]

‘ The whole play ’, Dr. Tillyard continues, ‘ is alive with the sense of creation's flux and not blind to creation's limit. Caliban may hover between man and beast, yet in the end he shows himself incapable of the human power of education. Prospero too learns his own lesson. He cannot transcend the terms of his humanity. In the end he acknowledges Caliban, “ this thing of darkness, mine ” : man for all his striving towards the angels can never be quit utterly of the bestial, of the Caliban, within him.’

Later, speaking of the influence of the Pythagorean doctrine on the great Elizabethan writers, he says : ‘ The Pythagoreans dwelt on man's unique comprehensiveness : he contained in himself samples of all the degrees of creation, excelling in this not only beasts but the angels, who were entirely spiritual beings. But it was not only a matter of including in himself these samples : man's very anatomy corresponded with the physical ordering of the Universe.’

He quotes from the *Life of Pythagoras*, by Photius, the Byzantine lexicographer, the following passage :

‘ Man is called a little world not because he is composed of the four elements (for so are all the beasts, even the meanest) but because he possesses all the faculties of the universe. For in the universe there are gods, the four

[1] My debt to this great scholar is here, as elsewhere, of the deepest.

elements, the dumb beasts, and the plants. Of all these man possesses the faculties : for he possesses the godlike faculty of reason ; and the nature of the elements, which consists in nourishment growth and reproduction. In each of these faculties he is deficient. . . .

' For we possess the faculty of reason less eminently than the gods ; in the same way the elements are less abundant in us than in the elements themselves ; our energies and desires are weaker than the beasts' ; our powers of nurture and of growth are less than the plants'. Whence, being an amalgam of many and varied elements, we find our life difficult to order. For every other creature is guided by one principle ; but we are pulled in different directions by our different faculties. For instance at one time we are drawn towards the better by the godlike element, at another time towards the worse by the domination of the bestial element, within us.'

In these passages, original and quoted, I believe this great scholar has discovered the true meaning of *The Tempest*. . . . Caliban, Ariel, are not only links in the chain of Being : they are also elements in the Microcosm that is Prospero.

As Dr. Tillyard says elsewhere in *The Elizabethan World Picture* (p. 60) : ' He ' (Man) ' was the nodal point, and his double nature, though the source of internal conflict, had the unique function of binding together *all* creation, of bridging the greatest cosmic chasm, that between matter and spirit '.

. . . .

' The real Archtypes . . . the eternal Ideas, the original forms of all things, can alone be said to have true being . . . because they *always are*, but never become nor pass away.' [1]

Coleridge, in his ninth Lecture, said that Shakespeare's characters, ' from Othello and Macbeth down to Dogberry

---

[1] Schopenhauer, *The World as Will and Idea*.

P

and the grave-diggers, may be termed ideal realities. They are not the things themselves, so much as abstracts of the things which a great mind takes unto itself, and there naturalizes them to its own conception.

'It is so with Prospero, Caliban, Ariel — although in the case of Prospero and Caliban, unlike the Archtypes of which Schopenhauer speaks, we see them in the process of becoming . . .'

The play begins with an upheaval of Nature, against which King and Common Man are helpless, — and with the casting of these beings (equal in their necessities, equally threatened by unknown dangers) on a strange shore . . . as we are cast on the shores of life . . . (the theme is a common one in Shakespeare). But it would be an impertinence to labour this point, or to dwell for more than a moment on the fact that here, as in *Hamlet* and *As You Like It*, there is the tale of a brother who had plotted against the brother who trusted him. (This theme, so often repeated, must, I think, have more than the obvious significance.)

Here, in this island upon which these beings are cast, are to be found the roots of Nature, the well-spring of all Being.

Prospero, although he is a ' masculine fire of Nature ', seems a being of the same order as the Semele of Euripides :

For her breath is on all that hath life, and she floats in the air
Bee-like, death-like, a wonder,

(Trans. by Gilbert Murray)

— a being with the grandeur of the lightning, with, occasionally, the sweetness of the Bee-Prophetesses, and with an anger like the

Hot splendour of the shaft of God.

When the enchanter, speaking of himself, says :

Prospero, master of a full poore cell,

it seems one of those double-edged remarks or puns which

occur so often in Shakespeare. The ' full poore cell ' is his
dwelling, but is also the cell of his brain, which should be
full and sweet as the cell of the honey-bee. But the honey
of his wisdom frequently turns sour.

> Thou shalt be pinch'd
> As thicke as honeycomb, each pinch more stinging
> Than Bees that made them (I, 2).

he says to Caliban.

And yet he is, I think, an abstract, an Archtype of the
Golden Race of Men, of whom Hesiod speaks, and to whom
Plato refers in the *Cratylus Dialogue* : ' I suppose that he
means by the Golden Men, not only literally made of gold,
but good and noble. . . . And are not the good wise ? '

Prospero, however, was not invariably good — his treat-
ment of the simple childlike savage Caliban was tyrannical
and cruel. He was not invariably wise — for he was an
experimenter with the Earth in the shape of Caliban ; and
in spite of all that can be said, he did not understand the
blind terror-striking qualities of the Earth. In the end of
the play, however, the Pride of the Intellect finds the path
to true wisdom, as, in *King Lear*, the Pride of the Body,
and of State, find their way to wisdom through the night
of the Soul.

When Trinculo, seeing Caliban for the first time, asks :

> What have we here ? A man or a fish ? Dead or alive ?
> A fish : he smells like a fish ; a very ancient and fish-like
> smell (II, 2) ;

— we are being given to understand that Caliban was
gendered between the earth and sea, in that part from which
all life began.

' The character of Caliban ', said Hazlitt, ' grows out of
the soil where it is rooted, uncontrolled, uncouth and wild,
uncramped by any of the meannesses of custom. It is of
the earth, earthy. It seems to have been dug out of the
ground with a soul instinctively superadded.'

But it was more than that.

When Prospero says :

> Thou Earth, thou ! speake (I, 2).

he is calling Caliban by his true name.   Caliban *is* the Earth — speaks with the voice of Earth.

So he is when in his natural state.   But under the tyranny of Prospero, the incomplete teaching of that magician, his nature changes from that of the noble earth to a being who is neither wholly earth nor wholly man — a being waiting to be remade by those false gods Trinculo and Stephano, into the image of the crowd — inspired by the crowd spirit to revolution.[1]

> You taught me Language ; and my profit on't
> Is, I know how to curse : the red plague rid you,
> For learning me your language (I, 2),

says Caliban to his master.

Ineffable prophecy !   Did some dark angel from three hundred years beyond his own death, come to visit Shakespeare ?

This is the secondary theme of the play — the revolution against the earthly order — mimicking the greater theme, the elements in Man warring against themselves.

Under false teaching, under oppression, the earthly order undergoes an upheaval.   And here again, in this secondary theme, we see the Chain of Being, the Principle of Order, broken.

Inspired by false gods, turned from his true nature, Caliban speaks with the very voice of the crowd :

> Ban, Ban — Ca — Caliban,
> Has a new Master — Get a new Man !

(a new Man, in truth !).

And

> Freedome, high-day ! high-day, freedome ! freedome !
> high-day, freedome ! (II, 2)

---

[1] See Note I on *Troilus and Cressida*, p. 152 *et seq.*

Through Caliban, speaks the material working power of the crowd, of the under-dog gaining the ascendancy over his master.

> Ile not show him
> Where the quicke Freshes are (III, 2).

The crowd has not changed. It is, now, what it was then. There is the same fear of that over-lord the mind.

The temporarily spoiled earth-spirit, speaking of Prospero, says :

> Remember
> First to possesse his Books ; for without them
> He's but a Sot, as I am, nor hath not
> One spirit to command (III, 2).

Many thousand years have passed since the fall of Troy, nearly three and a half centuries since Trinculo and Stephano had their being. But the dust in the common streets of the city is the same — now gold under the sun, now shuddering before the tempest comes. The mean and dirty dust of Pandarus, the filth that was Thersites, the base stupidity and cupidity of Trinculo and Stephano still have their being. But how different are they from the simple, fundamentally noble earth-spirit that is Caliban.

' That's not the tune ', he says suddenly (III, 2). Then from the mouth of the earth-spirit come these heavenly sounds :

> Be not affeard : the Isle is full of noyses,
> Sounds and sweet aires, that give delight and hurt not.
> Sometimes a thousand twangling Instruments
> Will hum about mine eares ; and sometimes voyces,
> That if I then had wak'd after long sleepe,
> Would make me sleepe againe : and then, in dreaming,
> The clouds me thought would open and shew riches
> Ready to drop upon me ; that, when I wak'd,
> I cried to dream againe (III, 2).

Here is the true earth-spirit, unruined by false civilisation.[1]

---

[1] In the first two lines, all floats in the air. Then, in the 3rd line, the sounds gain body with the *m* of ' Sometimes ', all comes to a central concentration with

*Note I. Certain Aspects of the Versification of
'The Tempest'*

Listen to the sea-enchantment of the sound of Prospero's
tale of how he and Miranda were cast

> To cry to the Sea that roar'd to us ; to sigh
> To the windes whose pitty, sighing backe againe,
> Did us but loving wrong (I, 2).

Here the beauty of sound is partly due to the particular
place in the line of the rhymes ' cry ', ' sigh ', and to the
contrast between the different lengths of the double-
syllabled words ' pitty ', ' sighing ', and ' loving ' — like the
sound of waves advancing and retreating and of the breaking of spray. This sound drifts along till it comes to the
wonder of

> Sit still, and heare the last of our sea-sorrow.

— one of the greatest miracles of sound in the whole of
Shakespeare.

It is not necessary to dwell more than shortly on the
influence that the masque in the Fourth Act had upon Keats.
It acted more, perhaps, upon his imagination and his voca-
bulary, than upon his actual versification.

The following was the ' sensual germ ' that, planted in
Keats' mind, led to many passages in *Endymion* :

> Ceres, most bounteous Lady, thy rich Leas
> Of Wheate, Rye, Barley, Fetches, Oates, and Pease ;
> Thy Turphy Mountaines, where live nibbling sheepe,
> And flat Medes thatched with Stover, them to keepe ;
> Thy Bankes with pioned and twilled Brims,
> Which spungy Aprill at thy hest betrims,
> To make cold Nymphes chast crownes ;   and thy
>   broome-groves (IV, 1),

' hum '; then the sound, which by now is fully embodied, drifts away again, and
mingles with the heavenly airs that inspired it.

Here, the wonderful use of a rhyme or assonance beginning and ending a line occurs again :

> *Ceres*, most bounteous Lady, thy rich *Leas*
> Of *Wheate*, Rye, Barley, Fetches, Oates, and *Pease* ;

the darker sound of ' Barley ' exactly balances the higher ' Lady ' of the previous line.

Notice, too, the beauty of the floating, far-off dissonances of ' pioned ', ' spungy ' and ' crownes ' — the sound of the latter deepening and concentrating into ' broome ', and this, again, to ' groves '.

The beauty is due, partly to the fact that in ' pioned ' the dissonance falls on the second syllable, and is unaccented.

Later, in these lines about Iris :

> Who with thy saffron wings upon my flowres
> Diffusest hony-drops, refreshing showres :
> And with each end of thy blew bowe dost crowne
> My bosky acres, and my unshrub'd downe,

— there is a lovely use of *s*'s and *f*'s — the first slowing the line in the slightest possible manner, the second giving a faint embodiment, — and great beauty is given by the fact that the lines ' flowres ' and ' showres ' are words of one syllable and a quarter of a syllable.

Note II

Dr. Tillyard, in an inspired passage of *The Elizabethan World Picture*, quotes the following passage from Raleigh's *History of the World* :

' And if we cannot deny that God hath given virtues to springs and fountains, to cold earth, to plants and stones, minerals, and to the excremental parts of the basest living creatures, why should we rob the beautiful stars of their working powers ? For, seeing they are many in number and of eminent beauty and magnitude, we may not think that in the treasury of his wisdom who is infinite there can

be wanting, even for every star, a peculiar virtue and opera-
tion ; as every herb, plant, fruit, and flower adorning the
face of the earth hath the like. For as these were not
created to beautify the earth alone and to cover and shadow
her dusty face but otherwise for the use of man and beast to
feed them and cure them ; so were not these unaccountable
glorious bodies set in the firmament to no other end than
to adorn it but for instruments and organs of his divine
providence, so far as it hath pleased his just will to deter-
mine.'

'Prospero', says Dr. Tillyard, a few pages after the
above quotation, 'is a man in whom reason is strong and
who both defies the stars when they are hostile and, when
they are kind, uses them to the general benefit. It is possible
that there is an intended connection between the stars and
Caliban's insusceptibility to "nurture" or education. The
stars, said Raleigh, had absolute sway over plants and
beasts. . . . Caliban is too much under the sky's dominance
ever to be other than he is.' [1]

---

[1] To Shakespeare, as to other great minds of his time, all the components of
creation seemed brothers under God.

Donne, in one of his sermons, has the wonderful expression :

'That glorious creature, that first creature, the Light.'

XXX

NOTES ON THE TEXTURE OF THE VERSE
IN ' CYMBELINE'

I HAVE already, in *A Poet's Notebook*, compared the different effects, produced by texture on the movement, to be found in two passages of *Romeo and Juliet* and *Cymbeline*.

If we examine this fragment of a speech of Mercutio :

> . . . True, I talke of dreames :
> Which are the children of an idle braine,
> Begot of nothing but vaine phantasie ;
> Which is as thin of substance as the ayre,
> And more inconstant than the winde, who wooes
> Even now the frozen bosome of the North,
> And, being anger'd, puffes away from thence,
> Turning his face to the dew-dropping South (I, 4).

we shall see that this air-borne music, whose miraculously-managed pauses — each like a breath of gentle air — are the result of the varying vowel-lengths, is very different from, is colder than, the lovely and wavering airiness of this speech of Iachimo's :

> The Crickets sing, and man's o'er-labour'd sense
> Repaires it selfe by rest. Our Tarquine thus
> Did softly presse the Rushes ere he waken'd
> The Chastity he wounded. Cytherea,
> How bravely thou becom'st thy Bed ! fresh Lilly,
> And whiter than the Sheetes ! That I might touch !
> But kisse : one kisse ! Rubies unparagon'd,
> How deerely they doo it ! 'Tis her breathing that
> Perfumes the Chamber thus ; the Flame o' the Taper
> Bowes toward her, and would under-peepe her lids
> To see the inclosed Lights, now canopied
> Vnder these windowes, White and Azure-lac'd
> With Blew of heaven's own tinct. But my designe,

To note the Chamber : I will write all downe :
Such and such pictures ; There the window ; such
The Adornment of her Bed ; the Arras, Figures,
Why, such and such : and the Contents o' the Story.
Ah ! but some naturall notes about her Body,
Above ten thousand meaner Moveables
Would testifie, to enrich mine Inventory.
O sleepe ! thou Ape of death, lie dull upon her ;
And be her Sense but as a monument,
Thus in a Chapell lying.   Come off, come off ;
(taking her bracelet)

As slippery as the Gordian knot was hard !
'Tis mine ; and this will witnesse outwardly,
As strongly as the Conscience do's within,
To the madding of her lord.   On her left Brest
A mole, Cinque-spotted, like the crimson drops
I' the bottome of a Cowslippe : Heere's a voucher ;
Stronger than ever Law could make : this Secret
Will force him thinke I have pick'd the locke and ta'en
The treasure of her Honour.   No more.   To what end ?
Why should I write this downe, that's riveted,
Screw'd to my memorie ?   She hath bin reading late
The tale of Tereus ; heere the Leafe's turned downe
Where Philomel gave up.   I have enough :
To the Truncke againe, and shut the spring of it.
Swift, swift, you Dragons of the night, that dawning
May bare the Raven's eye !   I lodge in feare ;
Though this a heavenly Angell, Hell is heere.
(Clock strikes.)

One, two, three ; Time, time ! (II, 2)

The movement, which is gentle and wavering like the flame
of the taper bowing toward Imogen, is the result of the
particular arrangement of the one-syllabled, two-syllabled,
and three-syllabled words : in several cases the line ends
with a three-syllabled word, which gives a flickering sound
to the line.

The texture is of an incredible subtlety.   The reasons
for this are manifold.   Sometimes it is due to the fact
that assonantal vowels, placed in close conjunction, are

embodied in consonants which have varying thickness or thinness (if we can apply the word ' embodied ' or ' thickness ' to the unbelievably air-delicate texture of the verse). The *ck* of ' Crickets ' in the 1st line undoubtedly gives the faintest possible body and roundness to the centre of the word, the *cr* and the *t* the slightest sharpness, — each of an entirely different quality (for the *cr* stings, while the *t* is sharp, but does not sting). ' Sing ' has a slight poignancy, owing to the *ng*, and is therefore longer than its assonance the first syllable of ' Crickets '. There is a tiny sharpening, again, in the second of these faint, dim assonances, ' The Crickets sing ' — because ' sing ' is a one-syllabled word.

Much of the beauty of the sound is due to the dissonance-assonance scheme that runs through it, and the rhythm, that lovely wavering movement to which I have referred, is, in part, the result of the arrangement of these, the way in which they are placed, sometimes close together (as with the small, dim, then sharpening sound of ' The Crickets sing ' and the bright *a*'s of ' Perfumes the Chamber thus ; the Flame o' the Taper ') and sometimes echoing the original sound after a space of some lines. An exquisite effect of dimming and brightening, brightening and dimming, is produced by the use of a vowel, first faint, then brightened, or vice versa, — or by the use of alliterative consonants followed by vowels that are, first bright, then darkened.

Here is an example of the former :

> . . . fresh L*i*lly,
> And wh*i*ter than the sheetes !

and of the latter :

> . . . ere he w*a*ken'd
> The Ch*a*stity he wounded.

When, for a moment, the thought of rape enters Iachimo's mind, with the creeping sound of

> . . . Our Tarquine thus
> Did softly presse the Rushes

there occurs the echo, 'fresh Lilly ' — ' fresh ' being an altered echo of ' presse ' and of ' Rushes ' — as if these two words were blown together and their changed sound had become a single entity.

> And whiter than the Sheetes ! That I might touch !

— ' touch ' is a hardened echo of ' Rushes '.

> But kisse : one kisse ! Rubies unparagon'd,

— ' kisse ' is a distorted dissonantal echo of ' presse '. We may notice, too, the change from the deepened, richened sound of ' Rubies unparagon'd ' through the dimmed ' How deerely they doo it. 'Tis her ', to the brightening

> . . . breathing that
> Perfumes the Chamber thus ; the Flame of the Taper

— this followed by the sound, flickering, bending and straightening, blowing faintly backwards and forwards like the flame, of

> Bowes toward her, and would under-peepe her lids

This effect is produced partly by the three dissonantal *o*'s that accompany the *w*'s of ' Bowes ', ' toward ', ' would ', and partly by the fact that, in the two words of the double syllables in this line, the first, ' toward ', has a second syllable that is accented and fairly long, while the second word, ' under ', has a first syllable that is, though accented, very slightly shorter than the ' ward ' of ' toward '.

. . . . . .

> One, two, three ; Time, time !

and almost as Iachimo's dark voice ceases, Time is abolished and we fall into a dreamless sleep amid the night airs. Then even the flickering taper, and its little movement that seems as if it were about to change into a sound, is gone, and we waken to find that the dark and faintly lightening, exquisite night-music has flown, and that we are listening to the sound

of fluttering wings wet with dew, to the sound of the music
that the clownish Cloten has brought into Imogen's ante-
chamber.

> Hearke, hearke! the Larke at Heaven's gate sings,
>   And Phoebus 'gins arise,
> His steeds to water at those Springs
>   On chalic'd Flowres that lyes ;
> And winking Mary-buds begin
>   To ope their golden eyes :
> With every thing that pretty bin,
>   My Lady sweet, arise :
>   Arise, arise !

Part of the beauty of that fresh, clear, and soaring movement
comes from the fact of the word ' Hearke ' being repeated
— (the first time is a kind of springing-board for the
second) — followed by its rhyme ' Larke ' in the same line,
and also because there are two breaths, two little flutters,
in the 4th line, between ' chalic'd ' and ' Flowres ' and
after ' Flowres '. The reason for the first flutter is that the
word ' chalic'd ' seems drawing itself faintly together, like
the calixes of those flowers when dew splashes upon them
(— this is caused by the narrow vowels). The reason for the
second flutter is that ' Flowres ' is a word of one syllable
and a fraction. The two flutters, therefore, move in a
different direction ; the first slightly backward, the second
slightly forward. The whole of the poem is really built
upon ' *in* ' sounds, sometimes sharp, as with ' sings ' or
' winking ', sometimes faint, as with ' 'gins ' or ' bin ', —
these alternating with poignant *i* and *y* sounds (' arise ',
' lyes ', ' eyes '). It is this, and the particular arrangement
of the double-syllabled and single-syllabled words, that
give the poem its lovely, incomparably fresh, springing
movement.

This is one of the few songs of Shakespeare that have
not been subjected, at one time or another, to wrong
printing.

XXXI

A NOTE ON SONNET XIX

THIS is one of the greatest sonnets in the English language, with its tremendous first lines :

> Devouring Time, blunt thou the Lyon's pawes,
> And make the earth devoure her owne sweet brood ;
> Plucke the keene teeth from the fierce Tyger's yawes,
> And burne the long-liv'd Phoenix in her blood ;
> Make glad and sorry seasons as thou fleet'st,
> And do whate'er thou wilt, swift-footed Time,
> To the wide world and all her fading sweets ;
> But I forbid thee one most heinous crime :
> O carve not with thy howers my love's faire brow,
> Nor draw noe lines there with thine antique pen ;
> Him in thy course untainted doe allow
> For beautie's pattern to succeeding men.
> > Yet do thy worst, ould Time : dispight thy wrong,
> > My love shall in my verse ever live young.

The huge, fiery, and majestic double vowels contained in 'Devouring' and 'Lyon's' (those in 'Lyon's' rear themselves up and then bring down their splendid and terrible weight) — these make the line stretch onward and outward until it is overwhelmed, as it were, by the dust of death, by darkness, with the muffling sounds, first of 'blunt', then of the far thicker, more muffling sound of 'pawes'.

This gigantic system of stretching double vowels, long single vowels muffled by the earth, continues through the first three lines :

> And make the earth devoure her owne sweet brood ;
> Plucke the keene teeth from the fierce Tyger's yawes,
> And burne the long-liv'd Phoenix in her blood ;

The thick *p* of 'pawes' muffles us with the dust, the dark

226

hollow sound of ' yawes ' covers us with night.   The music
is made more vast still by the fact that, in the 3rd line,
two long stretching double vowels are placed close together
(' keene teeth ') and that in the 4th there are two alliterative *b*'s — ' burne ' and ' blood ' — these give an added
majesty, a gigantic balance.

XXXII

SOME GENERAL COMMENTS

I

Of Shakespeare's Genius for Sound

COULD the infinite variation and fertility of his metrical genius be exhausted ? 'Music laughs at that as the sea laughs at palsy, as the morning laughs at old age and wrinkles. But a harp, though a world in itself, is but a narrow world in comparison with the world of a human heart.'—DE QUINCEY (writing of Mozart), *Theory and Criticism*.

II

Shakespeare's Apparent Irregularities

' Are the plays of Shakespeare works of uncultivated genius, in which the splendour of the parts compensates, if aught can compensate, for the barbarous shapelessness and irregularity of the whole ? Or is the form equally admirable with the matter, and the judgment of the great poet not less deserving our wonder than his genius ?

.   .   .   .   .   .

Are those very differences' (from the ancients) 'additional proofs of poetic wisdom, at once results and symbols of living power as contrasted with lifeless mechanism ?

.   .   .   .   .   .

' The spirit of poetry, like all other living powers, must of necessity circumscribe itself to rules, were it only to reunite power with beauty. It must embody in order to reveal itself ; but a living body is of necessity an organized one ; and what is organization but the connection of parts in and for a whole, so that each part is at once end and means.—This is no discovery of criticism ; it is a necessity of the human mind ; and all nations have felt and obeyed it, in the invention of metre, and measured sounds, as the vehicle and involucrum of poetry — itself a fellow-growth from the same life, — even as the bark is to the tree.

'No work of genius dares want its appropriate form — neither indeed is there any danger of this. As it must not, so genius cannot, be lawless : for it is even this that constitutes its genius — the power of acting creatively under laws of its own origination. How then comes it that not only Zoili, but whole nations, have combined in unhesitating condemnation of our great dramatist, as a sort of African nature, rich in beautiful monsters, — as a heath where islands of fertility look the greener from the surrounding waste, where the loveliest plants now shine out among unsightly weeds, and now are choked by their parasitic growth, so intertwined that we cannot disentangle the weed without snapping the flower ?

.   .   .   .

'Such as the life is, such is the form. Nature, the prime genial artist, inexhaustible in diverse powers, is equally inexhaustible in forms . . . and even such is the appropriate excellence of her chosen poet, of our own Shakespeare, — himself a nature humanized, a genial understanding directing self-consciously a power and an implicit wisdom deeper even than consciousness.'—COLERIDGE, *Lectures*.

III

Shakespeare as Idiot

'What ! Are we to have miracles in sport ? — Or, I speak reverently, does God choose idiots by whom to convey divine truths to men ? '—COLERIDGE, *ibid*.

IV

Writing for the Mob

Coleridge said : ' Nearly all they ' (the critics) ' can do is to express the most vulgar of feelings, wonderment — wondering at what they term the irregularity of his genius, sometimes above all praise, and at other times, if they are to be trusted, below all contempt. They endeavour to reconcile the two opinions by asserting that he wrote for the mob ; as if a man of real genius ever wrote for the mob.'

V

Of Shakespeare and Addison

'. . . The feeble constitution of the poetic faculty as existing in himself ' (Addison) ' forbade his sympathy with Shakespeare ; the proportions were too vast for his delicate vision.

' Those who have happened, like ourselves, to see the effect of passionate music and " deep-inwoven harmonies " upon the feeling of an idiot, may conceive what we mean. Such music does not utterly revolt the idiot ; on the contrary, it has a strange but horrid fascination for him ; it alarms, irritates, disturbs, makes him profoundly unhappy, and chiefly by unlocking imperfect glimpses of thoughts and slumbering instincts, which it is for his peace to have entirely obscured because for him they can be revealed only partially, and with the sad effect of throwing a baleful gleam upon his blighted conditions. Do we mean, then, to compare Addison with an idiot ? Not generally, by any means. Nobody can more sincerely admire him when he was a man of real genius, — viz. in his delineations of character and manners, or in the exquisite delicacies of his humour. But assuredly Addison, as a poet, was amongst the sons of the feeble, and between the authors of *Cato* and *King Lear* there was a gulf never to be bridged over.'—DE QUINCEY, *Shakespeare.*

VI

Of the Man Shakespeare

Before leaving these fires, like the multitudinous fires of the universe, lightning, warming, consuming, devastating, — like ' the fires beneath the earth, the immeasurable stars, and the great sun itself ', of which Pliny spoke, — the Tragedies where ' I meet not words, but thunder, and universal thunder, thunder that passes through the world ' [1] — the Comedies where the ardent harmony and ' the lightness and brightness of his fiery spirit ' [2] is infused into every particle of our human dust, we may pause to wonder why we know so little of the man, — of his parents, his brothers and sisters, his childhood and maturity.

According to a certain Archdeacon Thomas Plume, ' Sir John Mennis saw once his old Father in his shop, a merry-chee'd old man — that said Will was a good Honest Fellow, but he durst have crack'd a jeast with him at any time '. William Alderson tells us of one of Shakespeare's younger brothers, who lived to a good old age, ' even some years, as I compute, after the Restoration of King Charles II ', and who ' would in his younger dayes come to London to visit his brother Will, as he called him, and be a spectator of him as an actor in some of his own plays '. . . . But when he asked for memories of these visits, he, it seems, was so stricken in years, ' and possibly so weakened by

---

[1] John Donne, Sermon XLIV.
[2] Swinburne, on Nashe.

infirmities (which might make him the easier pass for a man of weak intellect), that he could give them but little light into their enquiries ; and all that could be recollected from him of his brother Will in that station, was the faint, general, and almost lost ideas he had of having once seen him act a part in one of his own Comedies, wherein, having to personate a decrepit old man, he wore a long beard, and appeared so weak and drooping and unable to walk, that he was forced to be supported and carried by another person to a table, at which he was seated among some company, who were eating, and one of them sang a song '.[1]

But what of the man himself ? Was he sweet ' as the honey of Hybla, my old lad of the castle ' ? [2]

James Joyce, in *Ulysses* (p. 185), speaks of him as ' Christ fox in leather trews, hiding, a runaway, in blighted tree forks from hue and cry, knowing no vixen, walking lonely in the chase. Women he won to him, tender people, a whore of Babylon, ladies of justices, bully tapsters' wives, Fox and Geese, and in New Place a slack dishonoured body, that once was comely, once as sweet, as fresh as cinnamon, now her leaves falling, all bare, frighted of the narrow grave and unforgiven.'

What remained to him, in his last days, of the dark beauty

> With Phoebus' amorous pinches black
> And wrinckled deep in time.

Was she, indeed, as Mr. Harrison suggested, a certain Lucy Negress ?

What were his agonies ? One can guess at them. But there is a great saying of Whitman which I think is applicable to Shakespeare : ' The depths are fathomless and therefore calm. The innocence and the nakedness are resumed.'

---

[1] See Sir Edmund Chambers, *William Shakespeare.*

[2] Gabriel Harvey tells us of ' old lads of the castell with their rapping babble — roaring boys '.

Perhaps all the agonies were set at rest.

Now, over his grave, the fires of his genius play, and like the countrywoman at Hockley, on a certain Easter morning, we may say to our fellow men,

Get up, get up, and see the Sun dance.

THE END

PRINTED BY R. & R. CLARK, LTD., EDINBURGH